A SIMPLIFIED INTRODUCTION TO THE WISDOM OF ST. THOMAS

Peter A. Redpath, *Ph.D.*
St. John's University

University Press
of America™

Copyright © 1980 by

University Press of America, Inc.

4710 Auth Place, S.E., Washington, D.C. 20023

ISBN: 0-8191-1058-2 (Case)

0-8191-1059-0 (Perfect)

Library of Congress Catalog Card Number: 80-5230

To my father, Joseph (r.i.p.) --

a wise man

ACKNOWLEDGEMENTS

There are a number of people who have, in one way or another, contributed to the production of this book. We wish to express our gratitude first to Dr. Gerald F. Kreyche for his charity and sound advice regarding the preparation and tone of this work; to Dr. Larry Azar for introducing us to the wisdom of St. Thomas; to Dr. Jorge J. E. Gracia for the model of excellence in research he has given us, and which, in our haphazard way, we try to follow; to our colleague Dr. David Winiewicz for his helpful comments about the manuscript; to Father Armand A. Maurer and to Dr. Henry B. Veatch for the insights we have received from them; and to Dr. Wilfrid Desan for his inspiration and counsel. In addition, we wish to thank Father Joseph Breen, Dean of Notre Dame College, of St. John's University, Dr. Thomas Houchin, chairman of the Humanities division of Notre Dame College, and our colleagues Dr. Augustin Riska and Professor Louis Weeks for their encouragement and help while we have been at St. John's. In addition, we wish to express our gratitude to our secretaries Diane Williamson, Kathy Monteverdi and Florence Carini for all the help they constantly give us. Finally, we wish to thank our wife Lorraine and children Peter, Paul and Korri for putting up with us while this book has been in the process of completion.

CONTENTS

PREFACE

The aim of this book is to provide readers and
students with a succinct and simplified introduction to
the philosophical teachings of St. Thomas Aquinas. We have
designed it to serve a dual function. We believe the text
contains a sufficient amount of information which readers
who have some knowledge of philosophy need in order to be
able to do their own research on St. Thomas. At the
same time, we believe that the text, also, contains a good
deal of significant material for anyone wishing to teach
an introductory course on Thomistic philosophy. In calling
it a "simplified" introduction we do not mean that it is a
"simple" introduction. All that we mean is that it is
simpler than most of the introductory texts one can find
dealing with St. Thomas's philosophy, and that the material
in it covers much of the basic information one needs to
know in order to do advanced research in St. Thomas's
thought.

In doing this work we have tried to write for a
general audience rather than for a specifically Catholic
readership, and we have tried to give, by and large, an
exposition, rather than a polemical defense, of St. Thomas's
doctrine. This attempt to open up St. Thomas's teaching
to a wider than normal audience has prompted us, at times,
to take liberties with the language normally used to
explain St. Thomas's doctrine. We do not think this excess
on our part will present great difficulty for those who
are familiar with St. Thomas's philosophy, and we think
it will be helpful for those who are just coming to learn
St. Thomas's thought. On the other hand, in our desire to
be succinct, we have, at times, kept our explications of
difficult points within very limited bounds. We hope
that this restriction will not cause great difficulty for
our readers, and we hope that any problems which might arise
in such cases are cleared up in other parts of the text.
In short, perhaps like any introductory text, this work
suffers to some extent from excess and defect. Our chief
hope is that these faults are minimal and that in what
follows we give a comprehensible and faithful rendition of
the wisdom of St. Thomas.

INTRODUCTION

St. Thomas - A Man Who Sets Things in Order
and Governs Them Well

At the very beginning of what may be one of his best works, G. K. Chesterton tells of a romance he conceived of writing. The work he envisioned is, in a sense, the statement we wish to make in what follows. Hence there is no better way for us to begin than by relating this story Chesterton never wrote:

> It concerned some boy whose farm or cottage stood on a slope, and who went on his travels to find something, such as the effigy and grave of some giant; and when he was far enough from home he looked back and saw that his own farm and kitchen-garden, shining flat on the hillside like the colors and quarterings of a shield, were but parts of some gigantic figure, on which he had always lived, but which was too large and too close to be seen.[1]

The condition of Chesterton's young boy seems to us to be the present condition of Western man, and of Western philosophy in particular, in relation to the teachings of St. Thomas Aquinas.

The West seems to be caught up today in a knowledge explosion. Yet for all the explosion of knowledge one would be hard-pressed to find any philosophical explosion of wisdom. Indeed, we seem faced with the paradoxical situation in which the more our knowledge increases, especially in the areas of experimental science and technology, the more our wisdom seems to decrease. We live in a world which, as many of us see it, divorces learning from living, a world in which facts have lost all value and values are not considered to be facts; in short, we live in a world which seems to have lost its sense of proportion and propriety.

1

The German philosopher, Martin Heidegger, observes that modern man has lost his sense of the word "being," and, that in so doing, may have cut himself off from the spiritual destiny of the West.[2] In effect, what Heidegger is saying is that modern man has lost his sense of reality insofar as he no longer understands what it means for something "to be." We could not agree with him more, and it is for this reason that we are writing this work on St. Thomas. For it appears to us that like the young boy of Chesterton's imaginary story, Western philosophy is looking for an effigy or a giant to wrest it from its dogmatic slumber. To us, St. Thomas is this effigy or giant, but he has been either too large or too close to be seen.

To put it in another way, the modern world is beset with a host of problems which modern philosophy seems quite incapable of resolving. This is not to say that there is nothing valuable to be found in modern philosophy. Far from it. Modern philosophy has uncovered a host of philosophical problems demanding clear-cut solutions. In addition, in areas like logic and language analysis, phenomenology and existentialism, modern philosophy has made important contributions to the history of philosophy. Nevertheless, it appears to us that, by and large, modern philosophy suffers from a major confusion which prevents it from developing those very principles which could help to resolve the most pressing problems facing Western man. For modern philosophy tends to confound philosophy and experimental science in much the same way that some medieval theologians tended to confound philosophy and theology.[3] In so doing much of modern philosophy cannot help but be a metaphysical wasteland.

It is precisely because of his penetrating metaphysical insight and because of his ability clearly to distinguish the nature of philosophy from other disciplines that we think St. Thomas is the best answer to the problems of modern philosophy. In addition, it is our firm conviction that no one in the history of philosophy had a better sense of order and discipline than did St. Thomas. Yet these are two of the elements which we find most absent from modern learning.

St. Thomas was fond of quoting Aristotle's description of the wise man as one who orders things rightly and governs them well.[4] At the same time, he referred to theology and, also, to a division of philosophy called "metaphysics," as a "wisdom." When we speak of the "wisdom" of St. Thomas, we are using the term primarily to refer to his teaching as a whole, not simply to his insight as a metaphysician.

One of the purposes of philosophy is ". . .to help us to understand things we already know, understand them better than we now understand them;"[5] but we think philosophy should do more than this. It should help us to become wise. Indeed, it is our firm conviction that St. Thomas is worth studying because we believe St. Thomas was wiser than any thinker in the history of philosophy. By reading him we believe one will be better able to ". . .order things rightly and govern them well."[6]

This means, of course, that we are writing for a special audience. This book is not for everyone. There are those, no doubt, who will think that such a call to ite ad Thomam (go to Thomas) ". . .would seem a call to inhabit once more a geocentric universe and a world of final causes where light bodies would tend toward the periphery and heavy bodies toward the center."[7] Some among these might be convinced that wisdom is impossible to achieve, or that if it be possible to achieve one would find it in the writings of modern or contemporary philosophers. This work is not directly intended for such people. Rather, it is intended for those who are convinced that the study of philosophy should make one wise, and who either have not studied philosophy to any great extent; or, if they have, have not found a philosopher who could satisfy their intellectual hunger.

It is because we are writing for a special audience that we have entitled this work A Simplified Introduction to the Wisdom of St. Thomas. No doubt there are some who will object to our attempt to present a simplified introduction to St. Thomas. For they will think that by simplifying his work we will be watering down his doctrine. In response to such criticism we can only say two things. One is that it goes against the spirit of St. Thomas himself not to share his wisdom with those who might be prepared to benefit from it. The other is that if one understands St. Thomas one should be able to make his doctrine intelligible to a general audience without doing violence to his doctrine.

On the other hand, there will no doubt be some who will object to our writing any introduction to St. Thomas at all. Their reasoning will be that as a Roman Catholic theologian, St. Thomas cannot speak to us as a philosopher. To such people we would say that St. Thomas was, indeed, a Roman Catholic theologian. This does not mean, however, that St. Thomas cannot speak objectively to us as a philosopher whose very faith inspired him to be as objective as possible. The fact that thinkers of the stature of Henry Veatch, Mortimer Adler, and Eric Mascall, none of whom is Roman Catholic, can be counted among the best of Thomas's modern interpreters testifies to his universal appeal. Of course, the best way to see that what we say is true is simply by reading Thomas. In so doing one will, we think, find that, for Thomas, just as grace perfects nature, so faith perfects philosophy. Hopefully, this work will enable some people to read St. Thomas and find this to be true.

PART 1

THE UNIVERSE

OF

ST. THOMAS

CHAPTER 1

A BRIEF BIOGRAPHY

The Young Thomas (1224-1239)

St. Thomas was the last son of twelve children born
to Landulf of Aquino, a lower nobleman whose castle was
situated in Roccasecca near Aquino, which is southeast of
Rome.[1] Thomas's father was married twice, bearing three
sons by his first wife, and four sons and four or perhaps
five daughters by his second wife, Donna Theodora, a
noblewoman of Norman origin from Naples. The exact date
of Thomas's birth is unknown, but reliable accounts put
his birth around the end of 1224 or the beginning of 1225.[2]

As Landulf's youngest son, the custom of the day
required that Thomas's parents dedicate him to the Church.
Today such a custom seems strange, but in Thomas's time
such a dedication would have insured Thomas's future. Like
any good mother, Donna Theodora wanted the best for her son.
If she were a contemporary mother she might want Thomas to
become a banker or a doctor; but as a thirteenth century
mother living in Catholic Italy, Donna Theodora could hope
for very little more than that her son would become Abbot
of Monte Cassino.

Consequently, after his fifth birthday Thomas was
brought by his parents to Monte Cassino as an oblate (one
offered to God) to receive training in the Benedictine life.
Thomas spent about nine years in the then relatively
peaceful background of the monastery learning the liberal
arts and the Bible. Just prior to his joining the monastery, Frederick II had been fighting with the papacy and
had held Monte Cassino under his control. In March of
1239 the Pope excommunicated Frederick, and fighting between the Emperor and the Pope was renewed. This circum-
stance precipitated somewhat Thomas's career as a Benedictine.
As a result of the renewed fighting between the Pope and

the Emperor, St. Thomas never received profession as a Benedictine. Instead, at the persuasion of the abbot of Monte Cassino, Thomas was sent to study at the University of Naples, an institution established by the Emperor ". . .to train shrewd and intelligent men for the imperial service."[3]

St. Thomas at Naples (1239-1244)

The fact that Naples was an imperial university is important because it means that the general atmosphere of education surrounding Thomas as a teenager was not theological in nature. The University of Naples was predominantly a law school founded by the king. At that time it was called a **studium generale** (a general house of studies). What Thomas studied here was primarily the liberal arts plus the natural philosophy and metaphysics of Aristotle. While the latter works of Aristotle were not yet allowed to be taught as part of the curriculum in places like the University of Paris, such was not the case in Naples nor in other universities of the Kingdom of Sicily. Naples was a center for Arabic translations in the early thirteenth century. Indeed, ". . .the whole breadth of Aristotelian science, Arabic astronomy, and Greek medicine flourished in Palermo, Salerno and Naples prior to their assimilation in northern universities."[4] Thus not only was Thomas introduced to the philosophy of Aristotle at this time, which he studied under a teacher named Peter of Ireland, but he was more than likely introduced to certain explanations of Aristotle's philosophy, called "Commentaries," done by Arab thinkers, in particular to those of a man who was then called "The Commentator"--namely, Averroes.

St. Thomas and the Dominicans (1245-1248)

The Order of Preachers had been established by Dominic Guzman in the early part of the thirteenth century. The formal establishment seems to have taken place in the year 1215 when Innocent III confirmed Dominic's request for an Order of friars which embraced preaching as its goal and study as its apostolate. As friars the Dominicans

8

did not take the vow of stability. Thus they could be transferred from one province to another by proper authority. In addition, they made their livelihood to some extent by begging for food and other necessities. Thomas came into contact with the Dominicans in Naples; this contact was to change in a radical way both the destiny of the Dominicans and the life of St. Thomas.[5]

We do not know exactly when Thomas was incepted into the Dominican Order (it appears to have been in 1244), but we do know his family was not pleased with his decision. It appears that Thomas's father had died in 1243. One can conjecture, then, that Donna Theodora was quite upset by Thomas's choice of a religious order. Certainly with his father dead, his mother must have felt more insecure than ever about the destiny of the family fortune. At any rate, after Thomas's inception Thomas accompanied John Wildeshausen, Master General of the Dominican Order, from Naples towards Paris via Rome. Thomas's mother seems to have directed his brother Reginald, then stationed with Frederick just north of Rome, to intercept Thomas and to bring him home. This he did with some difficulty; but the end result was that St. Thomas was forced to stay at home for about a year, during which he was able to read the Bible and do some minor work in logic.

The family fortune seems to have changed in 1245 when Frederick was deposed by the Council of Lyons. So, Thomas was released from captivity. In all probability he spent the next three years in prayer and study, observing the Dominican way of life.[6]

Cologne and Paris (1248-1256)

Student and Teacher

It appears that Thomas spent the next four years (1248-1252) in Cologne with Albert the Great, where Albert had been sent to set up a studium generale for the Dominicans. Albert does not appear to have been aware, at the beginning of their relationship, of the gifts of his student; by 1252, however, he recommended that Thomas be sent to the University of Paris for training as a Master in Theology.

The medieval university seems to have been modelled after the medieval guild. Like an apprentice the student was required to work under a master, who originally at the University of Paris, was a secular or diocesan priest. At Paris Thomas matriculated under Elias Brunet.[7]

The common practice in the medieval university was to have an undergraduate Faculty of Arts which prepared a student for further study. At the University of Paris the graduate faculties consisted of the Faculties of Law, Medicine and Theology. A student was usually admitted to the Arts Faculty around the age of fifteen. He was required to study for six years before obtaining a Bachelor of Arts. Then, after working under a Master on some classical texts, and after passing of examinations, the student was granted a right to teach the Arts (licentia docendi), and he became a Master of Arts. At about the age of twenty-one, then, a student could enter the Faculty of Theology. Here he was required to attend lectures on the Bible for four years, followed by two years of study of the Sentences of Peter Lombard. Having done all this, and having reached the age of twenty-six, the student received his Bachelor of Theology degree.

The student pursuing his Masters in the Faculty of Theology at the University of Paris had to complete three degrees: Biblical Bachelor (baccalarius biblicus), Bachelor of the Sentences (baccalarius Sententiarum), and Complete Bachelor (baccalarius formatus). After lecturing for two years on the Bible as a Biblical Bachelor, and, then, after lecturing for two more years on the Sentences as a Bachelor of the Sentences, a student could apply for his Complete Bachelor's degree. Upon achieving the age of thirty-four, upon fulfilling other requirements such as holding public disputations and begging the Chancellor of the University to leave to teach theology, the student could be granted permission to give his first lecture, his principium, and get his Master's degree.[8]

St. Thomas had already performed the function of a Biblical Bachelor while he was with Albert the Great in Cologne. Among the functions performed by a Biblical Bachelor, a most important one consisted of reading and paraphrasing difficult passages of Scripture by "running lightly" over the text. Thus a Biblical Bachelor like

10

Thomas was sometimes called a cursor biblicus (that is, one who "runs over" Scripture).[9]

When St. Thomas came to the University of Paris in 1252, he did so as a Bachelor of the Sentences. Thus he was required to lecture on this important work by Peter Lombard. One may well wonder why this was required. The answer lies in the fact that Peter's work was the most extensive and systematic collection of writings of the Church Fathers compiled up to Thomas's time. As such, the work was of major significance. The Church Fathers were men of eminent theological authority and orthodoxy who lived just after the time of Christ. They were either disciples of the Apostles or disciples of the Apostles' disciples. Because of their antiquity, authority and orthodoxy, they have always held a high place in the tradition of the Roman Catholic Church. The Sentences of any writer was a systematic collection of patristic writings, and it was used to probe more deeply into the mysteries of the Roman Catholic faith. Peter's collection was the best available to Thomas and his peers. Consequently, a Bachelor in Theology (baccarlarius Sententiarum) at the University of Paris was required to lecture of Peter's work.[10]

This method of reading texts might appear to some to be evidence of a lack of originality on the part of medieval thinkers. At the same time, it might serve to reinforce the notion stemming perhaps from the Renaissance that medieval education was a boring combination of logic chopping and theological indoctrination. While it may be true that the medieval method of teaching was later improved upon by some of the humanists of the Italian Renaissance, and while it may be true that some of the scholastic thinkers of the Renaissance were bores and dogmatists, academic freedom and originality were alive and well in Thomas's age.

The main problem thinkers of the thirteenth century were faced with was a lack of texts. They had no printing press. Because of a shortage of books, and to some extent because of the difficulty of the material, teachers were forced to read and to comment on passages from the work with which they were dealing. One must recall, too, that it was only around the start of the thirteenth century that

medieval Europe was beginning to come out of the Dark Ages.
The Church had made valiant attempts to preserve and promote
education after the fall of Rome, but continued barbarian
invasions throughout continental Europe thwarted her efforts.
It was not until Hugh Capet was able to restore royal power
in France in 987 that the tedious restoration of learning
in the West could begin.[11]

The reading of texts, then, (lectio) was one method of
teaching in the medieval university. As scholars became
more familiar with the works they taught, problems of
interpretation arose regarding difficult passages. Thus
from the reading there developed the disputation (disputatio).
There were two types of disputations held in the medieval
university. One was a formal exercise in class at which a
Master chose a thesis. Objections could be raised against
the thesis by the students or by the Master. A Bachelor
upheld the thesis by appropriate arguments and answered the
question. The Master had the right to intervene and the
final conclusion was his. The next day the Master could
take up the subject matter of the dispute; restate the
thesis; make a choice of arguments against it; announce
his own decision; justify it; and refute the objections.
If he wrote the lecture himself, the lecture became a disputed question (quaestio disputata). If a listener wrote it,
it became a reportation (reportatio). Twice a year, at
Christmas and Easter, a second type of disputation was held
for a general audience. A Master was free to hold one or
not and anyone could submit a question on any issue and
intervene at any time. Hence the name "quodlibetal questions"
(quaestiones quodlibetales), meaning questions on whatever
you please, became the name associated with these public
disputes.[12]

The disputed question became the distinguishing
feature of the medieval thinker's method of doing philosophy.
When applied to the writings of Aristotle, the disputed
question gave birth to Scholasticism in philosophy.
St. Thomas, together with many of his contemporaries, is
often referred to as a Schoolman or a Scholastic philosopher.
In so referring to Thomas, or to other thinkers, one should
be careful to understand that one is not attributing to
these thinkers a commonly held doctrine. The Scholastic
philosophy that St. Thomas engaged in at Naples and at
Paris was Scholastic in the sense of method and problems

considered. That is, the problems centered around the text of Aristotle and the answers issued from the disputed question.[13]

So much, then, for the training required for a Bachelor in the Faculty of Theology at Paris. Let us now consider what went on with Thomas at his first stay in Paris.

Since most of his Dominican predecessors as Bachelor of the Sentences had been in their forties when they came to Paris, and had been much better prepared than he, it is reasonable to think that Thomas was apprehensive about his ability to fulfill his assignment. In addition, it is reasonable to think that Thomas's probable apprehension would not have been alleviated by a warm reception from the Masters of Theology at the University of Paris. In the 1230's and 1240's resentment had been building among the secular clergy against the mendicant friars. For several reasons the Dominicans were looked upon with suspicion by the secular Masters. First of all, both the secular Masters and the French bishops viewed the friars as legates of the Pope charged with the task of Church renewal. Such fears were not groundless. Not only did the friars have supra-diocesan power to preach and hear confessions, thus overstepping the jurisdiction of the local bishop, but the Dominican Order was the first one in the Church to pursue preaching as its goal and study as its means, duties most closely associated traditionally with a bishop. In addition, in their early years at Paris the Dominicans manifested a greater concern for generating a large number of Masters in theology for the Church than they did for contributing to the self-interests of the members of the theology faculty at the University of Paris.[14] This distrust of the Dominicans was compounded by two events, one occuring in the 1230's and the other in the 1250's. During the 1230's, the University of Paris was allowed to have twelve chairs in Theology. The holding of a chair was important for influencing the policy, growth and direction of the University. As a result of peculiar series of happy coincidences the Dominican Order was able to obtain two of these chairs.

When the Masters at a medieval university wanted to redress a wrong they, like many of us, went on strike. In the guild-like situation of the medieval university, however, a strike by the Masters was considerably disruptive. When we think of a university today, we often associate it in our minds with sprawling buildings. Certainly the medieval university had buildings but very often a Master rented space near an administrative center and his students met with him in his quarters. Thus when a medieval Master went on strike, not only did he suspend all academic acts, but he also took his students and left town! One can imagine what kind of pressure such an event could put on an institution. From March of 1229 until April of 1231 the Masters at Paris left in a "great dispersal." The Dominicans did not join the strike and in the interim picked up one chair by succession and another by conversion of one of the secular clergy to the Dominican Order. When the secular Masters returned in 1231, they readily accepted the new situation, but in the 1250's they started to have second thoughts about the situation.

By the time Thomas arrived in Paris in the Summer of 1252, the conflict between the Dominicans and the secular Masters was gathering full steam. The previous February the seculars issued a statute restricting each religious Order to one chair. The Dominicans and the Franciscans refused to recognize the statute. Prior to March of 1253, the trouble was compounded by an incident involving four scholars and a companion and the nightwatchmen of the city. It seems that the latter had beaten up on the former and the Masters had received no satisfaction from city officials. In March of 1253, the secular Masters again went on strike. The two Dominican and one Franciscan Master of Theology refused to join them. The seculars responded by claiming that the Dominicans and the Franciscan, by refusing to strike, were helping to delay resolution of the matter. In addition, they expelled and excommunicated the mendicants from the "Consortium of Masters" ". . .until they swore to uphold the statutes of the university, particularly the statute of 1252, limiting religious Orders to one chair each."[15] Beyond all this the seculars forbade ". . .each Master from permitting the _principium_ of a Bachelor or himself attending it (unless he previously agreed to live by the oath to follow university statutes) or to permit him to lecture in effect."[16] Thus, in effect, the seculars were refusing to allow the granting of a degree of Master of Theology to any of the students of the mendicants!

One of the leaders in the anti-mendicant movement was
a man named William of St. Amour. He added fuel to the
fire by indirectly attacking the mendicants in a book as
ministers of the anti-Christ. Beyond that, in consort
with others, he was able to convince Pope Innocent IV to re-
scind all of the mendicants' supra-diocesan privileges.
Luckily for the mendicants, Innocent IV died two weeks
later and a Franciscan became Pope Alexander IV. Almost
immediately Alexander restored the rescinded privileges,
and, in addition, he ordered that the Dominican Masters in
Theology be restored to the Consortium. At about the same
time, Thomas entered the controversy by writing a treatise
Against Those Who Impugn the Cult and the Worship of God,
a defense of the friars against the harangue of William
of St. Amour.[17]

Thomas as Master (1256-1259)

In the midst of all this controversy, and with great
reservations on his part, Thomas took inception in Theology
between early March and mid-June of 1256. He was not
accepted into the Consortium of Masters for sixteen months,
after William's writings were condemned, and after
Alexander IV had written to William ". . . depriving him of
all benefices, excommunicating him, and placing all his
teaching and preaching under interdict forever."[18]

St. Thomas's personal title at this time was "Master
in the Sacred Page," and as the title suggests, he was
required to lecture on the Bible. In addition, during this
time he wrote several commentaries on Scripture and engaged in his famous Disputed Questions on Truth. Furthermore, he engaged in several quodlibetal questions, he
began work on his masterful Summa contra gentiles, and
wrote some important commentaries on Boethius.[19]

St. Thomas in Italy (1259-1268)

It is difficult to trace Thomas's life over the next
ten years. Between 1259 and 1261 he seems to have resided
at the Dominican Priory of San Domenico in Naples. Then

between 1261 and 1265, he appears to have been with Pope
Urban IV at Orvieto. Finally, in 1265 ". . .he was assigned to Rome to open a studium for the province. . . ."[20]
He stayed there two years and then went to Viterbo as a
lector on Scriptures for the Dominicans.

Two things of major importance happened to Thomas
during this period. First, he completed his Summa contra
gentiles, a work of major theological significance, and
second, he met William of Moerbeke, apparently at Viterbo.
William had a masterful background in Greek. He was so
skilled, in fact, that his translations are often used to
establish critical editions of the Greek text.[21] With
some encouragement from Thomas, William seems to have
increased his output of some work he had already started
on Aristotle. Certainly with William's help numerous
translations of Aristotle were made available to Thomas
between 1267 and 1272.

Thomas's Return to Paris (1269-1273)

Between the years 1269 and 1273 Thomas accomplished an
amount of work which Father James Weisheipl says ". . .de-
fies imitation."[22] What does Father Weisheipl mean? After
all, is not this rather extraordinary praise for one
individual to heap on another? It is until one stops to
consider what Thomas accomplished during this period. Not
only did Thomas have professional duties as a Master of
Theology at Paris, but he was in the middle of two major
controversies, one involving renewed attacks on the mendicants and the other involving a group of thinkers called
Latin Aristotelians, or Averroists. In addition to this,
". . .Thomas completed the entire second part of the Summa
and wrote part of the third; he wrote detailed commentaries
on all the major works of Aristotle, a number of important
treatises on polemical questions, and, numerous replies to
diverse queries."[23] Beyond this, Thomas had to spend
". . .considerable time in reading the works of other
authors, ancient and contemporary."[24] When all this is
taken into consideration, what Thomas accomplished over these
four years is astounding. All one has to do to see this is
to go to any good library and see the amount of writing
contained in the second and third parts of his Summa

16

theologiae and in his commentaries on Aristotle. All told, Thomas wrote about twenty-five pieces during this time totalling thousands of pages in length. It seems that all this was possible only by virtue of Thomas's enormous abilities of concentration, memory and contemplation.

Return to Naples and Death

Certainly Thomas's singular talents were recognized by many during his own time. By this time, for instance, he was a preacher general in the Roman Province of the Dominican Order. In 1272 Thomas was chosen to establish a house of studies in Theology at Naples. While there he seems to have lectured exclusively on the Psalms, and seems more and more to have been absorbed in contemplation.[25]

The combination of Thomas's deeper states of contemplation and his incredible workload seem to have culminated in a major decision made by him on December 6, 1273. During Mass he was struck by some wondrous occurrence which caused him to stop writing. The outcome of this event was that Thomas was constantly dazed (stupefactus). He was neither mentally nor physically able to write since, as he told his secretary, Reginald of Piperno, "all that I have written seems to me like straw compared to what has now been revealed to me."[26]

Not only was Thomas mystically absorbed by this event, he was physically ill after it. Nevertheless, he was called by Pope Gregory X to go to the Second Council of Lyons, to be held in May of 1274, to aid in reconciliation of the Greek and Latin Church. On the way Thomas took ill and asked to be taken to the Cistercian Abbey of Fossanova. He arrived there at the end of February and died on March 7, 1274.

Had Thomas known what was going to happen to his body at the hands of the Cistercians, one may wonder whether he would have chosen a different place to die. For almost immediately after its burial, his body began a journey of its own. Fearing that the Dominicans might steal Thomas's body, the Cistercian prior had his body moved from its original place to another sepulchre. Supposedly, after Thomas appeared to the prior in a dream the body was again

17

exhumed and returned to its original site, but only for a short time.

When Pope Gregory X died in the early part of 1276, the Cistercians feared a Dominican would be elected Pope. Thinking that such a Pope would force the Cistercians to return Thomas's body to the Dominicans, the Cistercians seem to have exhumed the body a third time and to have cut off its head. No doubt they were making a subtle distinction between one's body and one's head. This exhumation was followed by a fourth at which Thomas's mother was given one of his fingers, and a fifth one at which the monks at Fossanova ". . .seem to have boiled the flesh off the corpse, so that they could keep the bones in a small place."[27] "Finally, in 1369, . . .Pope Urban V ordered what remained of the body was to be given to the Order of Preachers."[28]

By this time the Dominicans were no doubt happy to receive any of the remains of Thomas. Happily, his writings have been preserved for us in a better condition than his body. Hopefully, as we exhume some of his thoughts over the next few chapters we will leave his doctrine more intact than his corpse.

CHAPTER II

PHILOSOPHY AND THEOLOGY

One of the major issues of the medieval period, indeed
perhaps the major issue which sets this time apart from
other periods in the history of philosophy, is precisely
the problem of the relationship between theology and
philosophy. The problem itself goes back to the very be-
ginnings of the contact between the Christian Apologists
and philosophy, and the whole scenario of events is no minor
one for philosophy itself. With respect to St. Thomas, the
problem is central. St. Thomas was first and foremost a —
Catholic theologian. When he philosophized he did so as a
theologian consciously believing that his Faith perfected
his philosophy just as grace perfects nature. No doubt
such a view appears strange to the modern philosopher who
tends to consider philosophy as ". . . something that is
done without presuppositions; the philosopher is one who
begins his task with a tabula rasa."[1] If such be the case,
how can St. Thomas be an objective philosopher? Would
not his Faith distort rather than perfect his philosophy?
We do not think so, but to show this it will be necessary
for us to consider what St. Thomas considered to be the
nature of philosophy and the nature of theology.

To do this let us begin not with St. Thomas but with
some rather common observations, the type which could
strike anyone about the knowing process. By doing this
not only will we begin to understand St. Thomas's view of
philosophy, but we will be able to appreciate, perhaps, a
little better the reasonableness of his view.

The Origins of Knowing

Each of us, at one point in his or her life, goes from
a state of ignorance, that is, from a state of not knowing
something, to a state of knowing what one did not know

before. We see this happening all the time. Most radically we witnessed it in ourselves as children when, after not knowing anything, we first came to know. In coming to know we notice that some things we come to know immediately, almost effortlessly, while other things take time to know and require a lot of hard work. Thus we distinguish between things we know immediately from things we know by study or investigation.

Next, we also distinguish between things we know by random and haphazard discovery from those we know by orderly and disciplined study. In addition, in the area of disciplined study we distinguish between those areas which are rigorously disciplined in the sense of being "scientific" from those areas which are disciplined areas of study but are not quite what we might wish to call scientific.

Certainly there is nothing odd, or unusual, or even unique about looking at knowing in this way. Not only does each of us appear to proceed in such a manner, but it seems necessary to say that knowing by study presupposes some kind of immediate knowledge on our part. For without such immediate knowledge on our part, it would be impossible to know by study. The reason for this would be that any one thing learned by study would have to presuppose some knowledge or some prior study. Certainly anything known by study does not occur "in a flash." Rather, it pre-supposes some kind of knowledge. At the same time, a person's first act of knowing as a baby could not be one which required some previous study by the child for then the person would never come to know.

Now there appears to be nothing odd, or unusual, or even unique about this view either. Indeed, this paradox seems to lie right at the heart of Plato's celebrated world of forms. For Plato saw no way to explain how people can go from a state of complete ignorance to knowledge. He thought that we all had to know something upon entering this life before we could know by study. Hence he at-tributed to man a prior life as a kind of god in another world where man knew everything.[2]

St. Thomas's Explanation

While Plato's view may seem far-fetched, it appears to us to be no more far-fetched than the view that there could be a presuppositionless philosophy. The reason for this seems obvious. Philosophy is not an immediate knowledge. It is a disciplined study. As such, it presupposes that we know something immediately and evidently. If we did not, no knowledge by study at all would be possible.

In a vague and general way, the view of knowing we have put forth contains St. Thomas's view of philosophy. For Thomas there is a difference between two ways of coming to know. One he calls discovery (inventio) the other he calls "disciplined study" or "discipline" (disciplina).[3] Philosophy is for Thomas a disciplined study which is demonstrative in nature. That is, it is a method of learning which is rigorously logical in nature. In a sense, then, for St. Thomas philosophy is simply learning by study in its most rigorous fashion.

Once we understand this, a number of problems become clarified not only with respect to St. Thomas's own doctrine, but also with respect to the history of philosophy. What we mean by the latter part of this statement is this: There has been a tendency within the history of philosophy to identify philosophy with a particular discipline of study--with theology in the medieval period, with mathematics for Descartes, with experimental science in the contemporary age. Such a confusion cannot help but follow when demonstrative learning is identified with the method of a particular discipline. This happened with the Church Fathers when they usurped for themselves the name "barbaric philosophers" because they thought they were answering the problems of the Greeks better than the Greeks;[4] it happened in the Western Augustinian tradition with its tendency to identify philosophy with a mystical discipline; it happened with the eleventh century's confusion of philosophy with logic and logic with grammar; and in each of these cases it happened, as it happens continuously, because of a confusion of scientifically disciplined study with a discipline of study.[5]

21

The Division of Philosophy

St. Thomas's conception of philosophy is, at its roots, Aristotelian. He distinguishes, in a fashion somewhat similar to Aristotle, between two general kinds of study. One called "speculative," the other called "practical." Once again, what Thomas is saying is not very difficult or unusual. Some things, he finds, we study just for the sake of understanding them. Other things we study because we want to do something with our knowledge. What distinguishes the one kind of study from the other is the motivating factor behind our study. In speculative study we investigate something simply to understand, for curiosity's sake so to speak. In practical study, on the other hand, we study in order to apply our knowledge and, so, to bring something into being.[6]

In either area of investigation one thing is certain. No significant progress is possible without the proper background. In neither area can one proceed from study to disciplined and demonstrative study without a mastery of some basic skills. For this reason, Thomas included the liberal arts among the things necessary for man to know. These skills--grammar, rhetoric, logic (trivium) and arithmetic, astronomy, geometry and music (quadrivium)-- ". . .are as it were paths (viae) introducing the quick mind to the secrets of philosophy."[7] They provide us with the method of demonstrative learning, and, in so doing, make the mind ready for other philosophical disciplines. These arts are philosophical disciplines, or divisions of philosophical disciplines, but they are "arts" as well because they involve not only speculation, but also some sort of work on the part of the mind. For instance, composing melodies, forming sentences, numbering things, or plotting the course of planets involves not only speculation about truth or falsity, but also some additional work of reason. Moreover, in order to be able to engage in more rigorous kinds of investigation, we have to possess the basic skills revealed by these arts. At the very least, we have to be able to read and write correctly; we have to be able to speak coherently and think consistently. In addition, a rudimentary knowledge of arithmetic and geometry is necessary to engage in higher mathematics, which, in turn is needed for "intermediary" disciplines, like

experimental science, which applies mathematics to
material occurrences. Finally, astronomy, which for Thomas
is ". . .one of the mathematical sciences, whose subject
is the heavens and celestial bodies,"[8] and music, which is,
also, an intermediary discipline (that is, one which applies
mathematics to the study of something material) are basics
which, like the other liberal arts, are called "liberal"
because they are studied not for the sake of some work done
by the body, but for a work of the soul. That is, these
arts are, likewise, called "liberal" arts, rather than
"mechanical" or "servile" arts, because the latter are
performed by the body which is, in a sense, related to man's
soul as a servant or instrument to a master. Since the
liberal arts involve work they are called "arts," but
since they do not involve servile work, what today we might
call "manual labor" or "technological application," but,
rather, intellectual work, they are called "liberal" or
"free" (liber). The reason for this is that, for Thomas,
man is distinctively free as a human being because of his
possession of a rational soul.[9]

The Division of Speculative
Science or Philosophy

Of the two major divisions of philosophy, by far the
most important for St. Thomas is the division of speculative
philosophy. For this reason, we will devote special attention to it here. However, to do this it will be necessary,
for us, once again, to start with a rather common observation regarding another paradoxical feature of human knowing.
We commonly say that when we most properly "know something"
we apprehend something truly. That is, we really know
something when we know it the way it really is. So in coming
to know, we go from not apprehending something at all,
or at least not apprehending it correctly, to apprehending
it the way it genuinely is. This poses a problem. For in
coming-to-know some kind of change occurs, always in us
and sometimes in the object. For instance, in eating a
piece of fruit we eat the fruit and both of us change, but
in coming to know a house, or a car or a bridge we change, but
the things do not. It is obvious, then, that in the knowing
process some kind of change in the knowing subject is always
involved. It is equally obvious that the kind of change

involved is, in a way, distinctively unlike the kind of change involved in eating. In the latter process the individual matter of the consumed object becomes the individual matter of the consumer, and in the process the consumed object is destroyed. The speculative knowing process is not one of destruction, however. It is, rather, for Thomas, one of liberation!

Here is a correlative problem. In order to know something truly, there must be some kind of identification made between the thing known and the knowing subject. That is, the thing known must be in the knowing subject, and it must be the same thing known which is simultaneously outside the knowing subject. For example, a piece of paper must, on the one hand, be outside of our mind in order for us to write on it, and it must be inside our mind in order for us to know it.

To put it briefly, then, the problem we are faced with is this. How can we know a thing in a way that is not "other than the way the thing is"? and, if we cannot know a thing in any way other than "other than the way it is," how can we be said to know something truly? For to know a material thing is to know it as material, but to know a thing as material appears to entail becoming materially one with that thing; which, in turn, appears to entail destroying the thing. On the other hand, not to become materially one with a thing seems to involve knowing a material thing otherwise than the way it is.[10] In either case, knowledge appears impossible to attain.

Perhaps, though, there is some way in which the mind can know a thing "other than the way it is" and, at the same time, not become involved in falsity. Thomas certainly thinks there is. To understand how this is possible it is necessary first to understand that knowing, to some extent, demands that the mind divorce itself from the individual material conditions of a thing. For Thomas, however, there are two ways in which the mind apprehends things. The first way is by simple apprehension (abstractio). In this way the mind acts as a recipient, and here the mind grasps, in some way or another, what the thing is. The second way is by a complex apprehension, by what we commonly call a "judgment," of by what St. Thomas calls "composition and division," or "separation" (separatio).

The difference between these two kinds of apprehension
is very important because it forms the basis of Thomas's
division of philosophy. Abstraction by simple apprehension
involves the simple consideration of one characteristic or
feature of a thing without taking into consideration some
other feature or characteristic. For example, when one
considers the color of an object rather than its shape, or
when an experimental scientist considers the chemical properties of something rather than its beauty. Beyond this,
abstraction by simple apprehension does not consider the
existence or non-existence of its object of study. It is
precisely this which distinguishes simple abstraction from
the complex abstraction involved in separation. By
separation, or judgment, we understand that one thing does
or does not exist, or does or does not exist in another.
There is another difference here, too. No error is involved
in simple abstraction when the mind considers one thing or
one aspect of a thing, without considering another. The
reason for this is simple. If a characteristic or feature
of a thing can be conceived apart from some other characteristic
or feature, our understanding or apprehension of the one
is not essential to our understanding or apprehension of the
other. For example, our understanding of the color "red"
does not depend for its intelligibility on our understanding
of the substance "apple"; so to think about the color "red"
without thinking about an "apple" does not falsify our apprehension. On the other hand, in the act of judging the
intelligibility of our judgment requires that we do not
judge to exist apart those things which exist united in
reality. In simple apprehension the mere fact that we can
form different concepts about things permits us to think about
them in isolation from one another. In judgment, however,
the mere fact that things can be conceived apart does not
permit us to consider them to be existentially separate. To
do so would be to falsify. The reason for this is that the
proper object of simple apprehension is the conceptual
property of a thing, what Thomas would call a thing's "essence,"
and the conceptual property of a thing can be understood
without reference to whether or not that conceptual property
exists, or without reference to some unrelated conceptual
property. The proper object of the complex apprehension
involved in judgment, on the other hand, is the existence of
a thing. So whereas in the act of simple apprehension one
has a _genuine_ apprehension when one grasps the conceptual
identity of a thing, in the act of judgment one has a genuine

judgment when one grasps the existential identity of a thing. Thus to separate in judgment what is not separate in reality is not to make a valid judgment, any more than to separate in concept what is conceptually united would be to have a valid concept.[11]

All this may seem quite puzzling to some readers, but it really should not. St. Thomas is not saying anything here which cannot be made clear. To make sure we all understand his point, though, let us go back and look at the example of the apple we just gave above. Suppose someone were to be particularly hungry, and he happened upon a nice, juicy apple. Seizing the apple, our friend proceeded to take a monstrous bite out of it, and then began to savor the taste of the apple. In so doing, he would be abstracting from the color of the apple, from its shape and so on. In fact, we might all agree that when we get very hungry the color and shape of what we eat is secondary to us. What we seek most is the satisfaction we get from the pleasant tasting qualities of the thing, etc. Nevertheless, even though we might not care about something's color or shape in one respect, this gives us no right to say that these same characteristics do not really exist in the thing. To put it rather briefly and somewhat vaguely, then, what St. Thomas is pointing out to us is this. By one kind of operation the mind apprehends characteristics or features of things. By a different kind of operation the mind apprehends the existence or non-existence of these characteristics in things. One should be aware of this and take caution so as not to confuse the two operations.

To get back to the question we asked a few pages ago, "Can the mind know a thing 'other than the way it is' and, at the same time, not become involved in falsity?" The answer is yes and no. If the phrase "other than the way it is" refers to the existence of the thing understood, the intellect is false when it understands, that is, judges, a thing to be other than the way it is. If, on the other hand, the phrase "other than the way it is" refers to the way we apprehend things, that is, to simple abstraction, there is no falsity in the intellect when it understands things other than the way they are.[12]

Now, let us consider how St. Thomas relates this distinction between simple abstraction and judgment to the division of philosophy. To do this let us consider the four basic divisions Thomas sees in speculative philosophy. These are: 1) natural philosophy or physics; 2) mathematics; 3) intermediate philosophy; and 4) natural theology or metaphysics.[13] One should recall that Thomas considers these four disciplines to be the major kinds of demonstrative learning available to man; and one should not feel perplexed if one finds these divisions odd, or if one does not quite understand the reason for them. We will try to make all this clear.

The immediate significance of Thomas's distinction between simple abstraction and judgment becomes clear as one sees how he differentiates one science from another. He says that, ". . .the speculative sciences are differentiated according to their degree of separation from matter and motion."[14] What does he mean by this? What he means is this: each science has a particular subject-matter and a particular point of view or formal perspective from which it approaches its subject-matter.[15] What distinguishes one science from another is not simply its subject-matter, but also the kind and degree of abstraction involved in the examination of its subject-matter.[16] That is, the subject of science is not simply a subject-matter; it is a subject-matter abstractly considered. It is precisely the kind of abstract consideration demanded by the thought object which divides one science from another. In short, the more one's understanding of an object depends for its intelligibility on individual circumstances and change, the less can one's understanding be called scientific or philosophical. Science is, thus, a way of understanding in some way abstracting from matter and change.

For Thomas, some of the things we think about are more dependent than others upon matter and change. "Some," he says, "depend upon matter for their being and for their being understood, ..."[17] For instance, suppose one were thinking about some particular individual, say a movie star or a T.V. personality like Cary Grant or Barbi Benton. Thomas would say, and most of us would agree, that in thinking about either individual we have to abstract from the individual sensible matter of each. That is, one's idea of either person does not contain that person's individual flesh or bone. Such a notion would be ridiculous; at the same time, one's idea of a human being would be deficient if it left out distinctively characteristic material attributes like flesh and bone. So, while forming a concept of a human being, we must abstract from the individual sensible characteristics or matter, of a thing, we cannot, as Thomas notes, abstract entirely from what he calls the "sensible matter," that is, the aspect of matter one can sense externally about the thing.

The kind of abstraction involved here is especially associated by Thomas with the natural philosopher or physicist. To understand why this is so, it is necessary to realize that when Thomas speaks of "physics" he is speaking in a more general way than we do today. For him, "physics" refers to a demonstrative study of the physical world from the perspective of its materiality and movement. It does not refer to mathematical physics which applies mathematics to its subject. The natural philosopher considers material things in abstraction from their individual distinguishing characteristics. He does not consider the individual as an individual, but as a material being of a certain kind. His approach is a little more general, then, than the approach taken by a person who simply has an experiential knowledge of a thing, or of someone who has a sense awareness of this or that particular thing. At the same time, his approach is not as general and abstract as that of a mathematician. The natural philosopher divorces himself from those particular "parts" of a thing which are unessential to his science. In so doing, he engages in a kind of simple apprehension which Thomas calls "abstraction of the whole" (abstractio totius), meaning that one examines the essense of a thing but not parts of a thing which do not belong to its essence.

The abstraction of the mathematician is, as we already noted, greater than that of the natural philosopher's. The natural philosopher abstracts from the individual sensible matter of a thing, but he does not abstract altogether from sensible matter. The mathematician, on the other hand, divorces his consideration not only from the individual sensible matter of a thing, but from sensible matter altogether. Note that we did not say he divorces himself from matter altogether, but from sensible matter altogether. There is a difference for St. Thomas. The natural philosopher does not divorce himself entirely from the sensible qualities apprehended by the external senses. He only

28

divorces himself from the individual manifestations of these sense qualities in particular individuals. The mathematician, however, separates himself entirely from the qualitative characteristics apprehensible by the external senses, but not from the quantitative characteristics apprehensible by the imagination. Thus the thought object of the mathematician depends upon quantified, or, as St. Thomas calls it, "intelligible" matter for its being and being known. Because, however, quantity does not depend upon sensible matter, that is, upon substance as subject to qualities and some other features, for its being known, the mathematician need not directly consider the sensible matter of a thing.[18]

In between the disciplines of physics and mathematics, Thomas locates what he calls an "intermediary science" (scientia media). Such a discipline is what today we might call "physico-mathematical." It is the type of discipline most of us today call by the name "science" or by the phrase "experimental science." This type of learning was just being developed in Thomas's own age in the fields of astronomy and optics.[19] Nonetheless, Thomas was acquainted with it, and gave, what appears to us to be an extremely perceptive and accurate description of its method. Perhaps the best way for us to show this is simply by quoting directly from Thomas on this point. Thus as Thomas puts it:

> . . .there are three levels of science con-
> cerning natural and mathematical entities.
> Some are purely natural and treat of the
> properties of natural things as such, like
> physics, agriculture, and the like. Others
> are purely mathematical and treat of quan-
> tities absolutely, as geometry considers
> magnitude and arithmetic number. Still
> others are intermediate, and these apply
> mathematical principles to natural things;
> for instance, music, astronomy, and the
> like. These sciences, however, have a
> closer affinity to mathematics, because in
> their thinking that which is physical is,
> as it were, material, whereas that which is
> mathematical is, as it were, formal. For
> example, music considers sounds, not inas-
> much as they are sounds, but inasmuch as

they are proportionable according to numbers; and the same holds in other sciences. Thus they demonstrate their conclusions concerning natural things, but by means of mathematics. Therefore nothing prevents their being concerned with sensible matter insofar as they have something in common with natural science, but insofar as they have something in common with mathematics they are abstract.

Each of the sciences--physics, mathematics, intermediate science and metaphysics--uses simple apprehension. However, metaphysics, or natural theology, also involves the use of speculative judgment, that is, **separatio**. Perhaps the easiest way to understand why Thomas attributes this additional operation to metaphysics consists in reviewing for a moment the general subject-matter of some of the different sciences. Both natural philosophy and mathematics apprehend characteristics or features of a thing. In other words, they grasp **what** a thing is either essentially or in some other respect. The natural philosopher considers **what** a thing is by divorcing himself from those characteristics which are not essential to a species (i.e., by abstractio totius). The mathematician considers what a thing is quantitatively by abstracting from other features or forms which are not essential to that thing as quantitative. Thus he does not abstract the essence from its individuals, like the natural philosopher. Rather, he abstracts one non-essential feature from other non-essential features, quantity from quality and other features (for this reason Thomas calls this abstractio formae). Metaphysics, on the other hand, has as its subject-matter not the essential or quantitative characteristics of a thing. Its subject-matter is the existential character of being. That is, it studies **what is** from the perspective of what is most fundamental and perfect in reality.[20]

No doubt all this is rather confusing to someone who has never been exposed to it before. To clear up any difficulties, let us try to simplify what Thomas is saying. Recall for a moment our explanation above about the two different ways we come to know things. One way we said was immediate, requiring no prior foundation in knowledge. The other way was by study, and requiring a foundation in some immediate knowledge. What is this knowledge? What is its proper subject-matter? These are the questions which one might say are the starting points of metaphysical learning.

Note that each of the sciences has certain starting points which are the source or background of all our knowledge in a certain area. St. Thomas calls these starting points "principles" of knowledge because our knowledge has its source in them and originates from them. For instance, the starting point of natural philosophy is the essence of a thing abstracted from individuals. It is that upon which all our knowledge of material and changeable being depends as material and changeable. Hence the natural philosopher must continually refer to the nature of a thing to explain the causes of material operations and change. The starting point of mathematics, on the other hand, is not the essence of a thing, but the essence as quantified. Thus quantified being is the source of all of our knowledge of mathematics. Hence the mathematician must continually refer to imaginative aids to get his point across.

Our source of knowledge in each of these areas is something which is in one way or another. To put it in another way, both natural philosophy and mathematics study the requisite features for being in a certain way. Metaphysics, on the other hand, examines the requisite features for being at all.

The problem which Thomas is faced with here is that of discovering by disciplined study what it is that the mind knows immediately when a person first comes to know. What he seeks to penetrate is the most intimate source of a thing's power of operation, the starting point of its reality as an existing nature. What he realizes almost instantly is that the mode of abstraction proper to sciences which grasp ways of being are inadequate when confronted with a subject-matter as simple as being in general (ens commune). What Thomas wants to know is what makes any and everything to be real, not what makes a thing to be real in this or that way. Since, in our usual attitude of knowing, we do not deal with questions like this (we deal rather with questions like what makes this to be this kind of thing rather than that), Thomas understands that in doing

31

metaphysics one must reverse what one might call the "natural attitude" of study. This is precisely why he brings up the second kind of apprehension which he calls judgment or separation. There is nowhere in the notion of being anything which demands that we understand being as material or as quantitative. Hence the metaphysician can consider a thing insofar as it is, just as a natural philosopher can consider a thing as material, and a mathematician can consider it as quantitative; and this means that a metaphysician abstracts not only from quantity but also from matter and change. The things he studies depend on matter neither for their being nor for their being known.

Since the metaphysician studies things which can exist or actually do exist without matter, Thomas can quite easily study not only objects like being and attributes common to all things, but also beings like God and angels. Needless to say, many people may find this disturbing. Nevertheless, all this seems quite consistent with Thomas's principles.

Metaphysics--The Highest Degree Intellectual

After going over what Thomas says about the different speculative sciences, it should be obvious that Thomas considers there to be an order and hierarchy in knowing. He thinks that one speculative science is higher than another. Since this is a point which we think some readers may find perplexing, we should try to make clear what Thomas means in speaking this way, and why his view is a reasonable way to look at the situation.

To do this consider for a moment the different ways we know things and the reasons we give for calling someone "intelligent." All of our knowledge starts in the senses, but we do not call someone "smart" or "wise" because he can distinguish between blue and brown, or between sweet and sour. In general, we consider mathematics harder than merely sensing something because mathematics is more abstract and because its object is less readily available to contact with our senses. In a way, then, we consider a study more difficult and higher to the extent that its subject-matter is more remote from penetration by our senses, and to the extent that the degree of abstraction required is more intense. In addition, we consider something to be harder to understand than another if, in order to know the former, one must first know the latter.

It is precisely for these three reasons that St. Thomas considers metaphysics to be the highest of all the speculative sciences. He is not making a moral judgment on the matter. He is simply stating what appears to be an obvious fact. He thinks a study is more intellectual than another for any of the following reasons: 1) its object is more remote from sensation; 2) the operation of the intellect is more abstract; or 3) the order of knowing is more basic. In all three cases, however, metaphysics is, for him, the highest degree intellectual: First, because it studies being from the perspective of being rather than from the perspective of being material or being quantitative; and secondly, because it requires not merely abstraction on the essential level, but a reversal of this natural attitude in an existential judgment. Finally, because in the order of knowing it examines the sources of all human knowledge, not simply the sources of knowledge in a certain area.[21]

Recognizing all this Thomas compares the different methods of reasoning involved in the speculative sciences in the following way. Natural philosophy, he says, proceeds most like reasoning (rationabiliter) because it proceeds most like our usual attitude in knowing things. That is, it starts with the senses and generates thinking and investigation. Mathematics, on the other hand, proceeds most like a discipline (disciplinabiliter) because more than any other science it generates certainty which is the end of learning (disciplina). Finally, he says, metaphysics proceeds most like understanding (intellectualiter) because its method of reasoning most closely approaches immediate apprehension, the method of knowing proper to the intellect.[22]

St. Thomas and Theology

Having gone over, to some extent, Thomas's view of philosophy, it is difficult to see how one could say his

thinking has been corrupted by his theology. Especially
if one takes metaphysics to be a prime example of
philosophy, it would appear that Thomas was aided,
rather than hindered, by being a theologian. For in
theology and in metaphysics (St. Thomas sometimes, also,
calls this "first philosophy" or the "divine science"),
the procedure is somewhat similar. As St. Thomas himself
notes, "The knowledge of faith also belongs in a special
way to understanding (intellectus). For we do not possess
the things of faith through the investigation of reason,
but we hold them by simply receiving understanding."[23]
In other words, the metaphysician must be extremely
cautious on the level of immediate knowledge. For where
he is likely to make his biggest mistake is right at the
beginning. So conscious was Thomas of this fact that he
begins his first metaphysical work, a masterful piece
called On Being and Essence, with the following statement:
"A slight initial error eventually grows to vast proportions,
according to the Philosopher."[24] Yet it appears to us
that Thomas's profound metaphysical insight, his central
philosophical intuition, arose from his intense grasp of
Catholic theology.

Of course, what we say here may sound strange to many
readers. The reason for this, however, may lie in what we
see as a tendency for the modern age to identify Faith
with a blind adherence to doctrine, and theology with
opinions about what one should believe. St. Thomas, however had a radically different view of theology and of
religious Faith. The medieval period was a profoundly
mystical age. Thomas, himself, was steeped in this
mysticism. He was greatly influenced by the mystical
writer Dionysius the Areopagite, so much so that the theme
of his inaugural address (principium) as a Master in
Theology ". . .was the Dionysian principle that divine
providence has ordained all higher gifts, both spiritual
and corporeal, to descend from the highest even to the
lowest through intermediaries."[25] In addition to this,
one can see the same principle lying behind the structure
of both the Summa contra gentiles and the Summa theologiae.

Religious Faith, therefore, for Thomas, is not a
blind adherence to law. It is knowledge of mystery, of
that which surpasses the natural power of the human intellect.[26] As such, it is much more like a mystical insight

34

that a sheepish and uncritical acceptance. The man of Faith is, for Thomas, a man of wisdom.

To see more clearly why he thinks this, perhaps it will be best for us to contrast the roles of the metaphysican and the Catholic theologian. For Thomas metaphysics is not simply a science of being from the perspective of its requisite features. It is primarily the science which studies God to the extent that man can know God by reason. Of course, Thomas does not think that man can know much about God. At best, man can attain to some kind of vague and indirect knowledge of God through His creation. Yet he thinks that the little bit that can be known about God ". . .is loved and desired more than all the knowledge that we have about less noble substances."[27] Certainly man cannot comprehend the mysterious nature of God. What God is is totally incomprehensible to man.

This, of course, presents a problem. Man's highest happiness, for Thomas, lies in knowing God. This is a goal, however, which exceeds the limits of human reason. How, then, can man ever learn to order his actions to achieve this end? To say simply that one can come to know that man has God as an end does not seem to be enough to lead man to God.

Thomas's answer is that where reason is no longer able to understand, the role of Faith comes in. For this reason, Faith does not oppose reason; it perfects it. Faith implants in man the conviction that the source of his happiness lies in something incomprehensible to man, and that any attempt to comprehend this end by light of reason alone is doomed to failure. As Thomas sees it, if the end of man (that is, man's cause and fulfillment) is incomprehensible, Faith is a necessary condition for man's happiness.[28] Not only that, with Augustine and Varro, Thomas thinks, "There is no other reason for a man philosophizing except to be happy."[29] Hence, not only does Faith perfect human life, it perfects philosophy.

In talking about Thomas's view of Faith one should be careful not to confuse Faith and theology. Theology, for Thomas, is the science of revelation. The job of the theologian is to explain by reason what has been revealed by God to man because what has been revealed by God is

necessary for human happiness. Does this mean that it is
the job of the theologian to explain the mysteries of
Faith? No! It is simply his job to point out what
mysteries are proposed to man for his belief. Unlike
some thinkers, Thomas does not identify revelation with
that which is incomprehensible. For Thomas certain parts
of theology are purely rational. The science of revelation
contains not only mysterious elements, elements which had
to be revealed (<u>revelatum</u>), it also contains elements
which are non-mysterious, things which are not beyond the
scope of human reason, but which were revealed because
they are difficult for man to learn. These things he
calls "revealable" (<u>revelabilia</u>).[30]

   To sum up the point we have been trying to make in this
chapter, for Thomas there is no conflict between theology
and philosophy. The mysterious aspects of revelation are
beyond the scope of demonstrative learning. For this reason,
they cannot conflict with it. At the same time, any attempt
to demonstrate the truth or falsity of a religious mystery
is a piece of sophistry. It is precisely because he looks
at theology the way he does that Thomas can be such a
critically objective philosopher. He does not use philosophy as a crutch for his Faith or as an apologetic. Rather,
he uses his Faith to guard his philosophy against presumption.

CHAPTER III

ST. THOMAS AND ARISTOTLE

To understand the universe of St. Thomas it is necessary to have some familiarity with certain views Thomas inherited from Aristotle. For not only does Thomas employ some of these views time and again, but some of the things Aristotle held posed problems for St. Thomas.

To begin with, Aristotle had held a five-fold division or order in the physical world. He divided physical things into five main classes: elements, composites, plants, animals and man; and both he and St. Thomas considered these classes to be related in a hierarchial way. Man occupies the highest place in the order of nature followed respectively by animals, plants, composites and elements.

Once again, some readers might find this perplexing. So, let us pause for a moment to explain the reasons Thomas and Aristotle adopted this view. They were not making a moral judgment or expressing some kind of personal preference. All they were doing was recognizing what appears to be a rather obvious fact. Certain physical bodies closely resemble other physical bodies in their appearance, in their behavior, in their control by their environment, and in their ability to exert an influence on others. Most of us, for instance, have little trouble distinguishing a rock from a plant, or a plant from an animal, or an animal from a man. Stones certainly, in general, look more like other stones than they look like people. At the same time, stones behave differently than do plants, animals or people. We do not expect them to drive to work in the morning, or to get married, or to raise a family. Furthermore, they do not seem to have much control over their destiny. They do not grow, they do not move from one place to another, unless moved by man, machine or mother nature. And, in general, they exert a rather uniform influence on others. We need rock to build homes on, but we do not fear being bitten by a stone or being arrested by a piece of slate.

Plants, on the other hand, behave more independently than do stones. Unlike the stone, which is a composite of lifeless elements, the plant is alive. There is some power within it which enables it to have greater say than has the rock over what it will become. It undergoes nutrition, growth and reproduction; and, thereby, exerts an influence on its environment, and acts with a certain autonomy.

Unfortunately, however, the plant cannot, of its own volition, just get up and move to a new location. It is rooted in the ground. The animal does not have this problem. It can walk, or swim, or fly away if it so chooses. Physically, animals tend to be more powerful than plants. They have feet, or hands, or wings which give them a say in what is to become of them. They behave more autonomously than plants, and are able to exert a wider influence on others than plants.

Of all kinds of physical things the most free is man. For the criterion which Aristotle and St. Thomas use to determine the hierarchy of nature is precisely the freedom proper to certain kinds of physical things. One kind of thing is higher than another precisely because it is freer in its operation.

All this seems so rather obvious that one wonders why anyone would have trouble accepting it. Of course, we do, at times, have trouble determining just what level of reality is occupied by a particular thing, but does not this simply reinforce the fact that Aristotle and Thomas are right in distinguishing among different levels of reality? For even if the distinctions are, at times, not clear-cut or even very rigid, the mere fact that we have trouble classifying them indicates we tacitly accept a difference in classes.[1]

Essence and Accident

What is it which enables us to distinguish one level of physical being from another? It is some kind of awareness of what Aristotle called the "essence" of the being. Today, we might call this the "distinguishing feature" of something. The essential characteristic of a thing, then, is simply a feature which is found on some levels of being but not in others. For instance, the power to sense in animals, and the power to deliberate in man are distinguishing features because they are found in some kinds of physical things but not in others.[2]

Aside from the distinguishing features there are other kinds of attributes, what we might call "differentiating features," which enable us to separate in a less radical way, one thing from another. Such characteristics Aristotle referred to as "accidents." Such features can be found on any level of physical nature, may belong to a thing sometimes but not at others, and may belong to some things on the same level of nature but not to others.[3]

Aristotle himself gave a list of the different kinds of features attributable to any physical thing on any level of nature. The general name given to this list is that of "categories." The categories themselves consist of ten divisions which run as follows: substance, quantity, quality, relation, position, place, time, action, passion and possession.[4]

What separates one level of reality from another is, then, a substantial characteristic, and, as such, it cannot be a quantity or a quality, a relation or any of the other differentiating accidents. For example, a human being is distinguished from an animal by a power not possessed by any lower level of physical reality, namely by his power to know. Thus we are not entitled to dismiss someone from membership in the human species because of his color (quality), or because of his size (quantity), or because of his geographical origin (place).

The Three Conditions of Physical Change

One of the other things Thomas inherited from Aristotle was Aristotle's principles of physical change. One might say that the problem of change was the central problem of Greek philosophy from its beginning up to Aristotle. In order to explain how physical change occurs Aristotle found it necessary to point out the three essential ingredients he found working in every changing nature. He called these matter, form and privation. In order to understand this point, we have to update his language a bit, and we have to be careful not to read into his explanation meanings he did not intend. First of all, Aristotle uses the term matter here in a wider sense than we do. We tend to think of matter as something "hard" or as something quantitative. When Aristotle and St. Thomas think of it they tend to look at it as a conductor or receiving force. The matter that Aristotle is talking about here is what we might call an "underlying subject" or a "subject-matter." Secondly, when we think of something's form, we tend to think of its shape. While St. Thomas and Aristotle do not have an identical conception of form, both tend to view it as an active force, or what we might call a feature. Finally, the term "privation" refers to a lack on the part of a subject of some feature it can possess.

Given these initial qualifications, when Aristotle speaks of the three conditions of physical change what he is talking about is this. For there to be any physical change there must be 1) a subject undergoing the change; 2) a feature that the subject can receive; 3) the absence in the subject of the particular feature it is going to receive.[5]

Thus what Aristotle is saying seems rather common-sensical; but to make the point clear let us give a practical example. Suppose you were to pick up a magazine advertisement for a weight-reducing plan. On one side of the ad (the "Before" side) was a picture of a football player, say of Roosevelt Greer, and on the other side (the "After" side) was a picture of Twiggy. Would you go out and buy such a plan? Obviously not, but why? Simply because any real physical change demands that there be the same subject-matter before and after the change.

Two different features with no subject, or one subject with the same feature before and after simply is not intelligible on the level of physical change.

The Four Causes of Change

Aristotle recognized that his three conditions of change were not enough to give a complete explanation of physical change. To have a complete understanding of physical change Aristotle thought one had to know not only the underlying subject of the change (material cause) and the feature the subject was to receive (formal cause), one also had to know the force behind the change (efficient cause) and the direction of the change (final cause - that is, either the intention of the agent if the efficient cause be a person, or the characteristic way of behaving imparted to the effect if the cause be inanimate). For example, suppose someone happened upon something like a pen for the first time. To give such a person an adequate understanding of such a being, Aristotle would consider it sufficient to say that the pen was an instrument or tool (formal cause) made of plastic, rubber, metal and ink (material cause), made for writing (final cause) by such and such a company (efficient cause). Suppose on the other hand, the same person experienced a rain-soaked street for the first time. To give him an adequate explanation of such a phenomenon Aristotle might say that the pavement (material cause) which was not wet before (privation) became wet (formal cause) as a result of chemical changes in the atmosphere (efficient cause), and that, as a result, the street is slippery and cool (final cause).[6]

A Problem With Aristotle's View of Change - The Perpetual Existence of the World

From the above examination one might think Thomas would have no difficulty with Aristotle's view of change. Such is far from the case however. Actually the reason for this is easy to see. Both Aristotle and St. Thomas are dealing with different problems. As a Greek philosopher Aristotle inherited the problem of change passed down from the pre-Socratics. To put it briefly, that problem was this,

"What is the basic raw material out of which all things are made, and how did everything get to be the way it is now from this first basic material?" To answer this question Aristotle conceived of physical things as a combination of two basic forces--a passive force, which acted like a conductor, which he called "matter" or "potency," and an active force, which gave matter its definiteness or feature, which he called "form" or "act." To give a kind of vague example of what Aristotle was thinking, consider the way certain substances are able to conduct certain kinds of features. For example, water and copper are good conductors of electricity, and paper is a good conductor of fire. Paper, on the other hand, is a poor conductor of electricity, and neither water nor copper burst into flames when they come into contact with fire. Why the difference? Why, for instance, do we watch shows on T.V. and not on light bulbs? The answer is obvious, one subject-matter has an ability to conduct a feature while the other subject-matter does not. The same fire and electricity are manifested in different ways in diverse things because of the conducting power of the receivers. Matter, for Aristotle and for St. Thomas, acts in the same way. It is a receiving or conducting power. A better way of putting it, perhaps, is to say that the basic raw material of the physical world consists of a multiplicity of underlying subjects or conductors (matter) and diverse types of distinguishing and differentiating features (form) which combine in different ways or proportions throughout the course of time. Each physical thing then, is a product resulting from the combination of these two complementary powers, which unite according to their compatability for one another.[7]

The major point we wish to make about Aristotle's view of the composition of physical things, and about his view of the three conditions of change is this. These views arise within the context of the thoroughly ancient Greek attitude that the universe is perpetually existent. The early Greeks tended to view the world as flowing by necessity out of some basic raw material. For them the world always was and always will be. What is here now simply came from something which was here before. All they wanted to know, then, basically was what was the nature of the basic stuff which was continually being rearranged to form the variety of things they found around them.[8]

42

It should be obvious that St. Thomas's world view as a Catholic theologian had to differ quite radically from the way Aristotle was disposed to see the origin of things. If everything which is now simply came from something which was here before, what are we to make of the Judaeo-Christian account of creation?

This issue was hotly disputed during the medieval period. On the one hand there were those who believed, as St. Bonaventure did, that one could demonstrate that world had a beginning in the past. On the other side there were those, following Averroes, who held that the world was demonstratively without beginning in the past. In the middle stood St. Thomas. Basically his position was this. There is nothing contradictory in the notion of perpetually existent universe. Nor is there anything heretical in the belief that God could have created such a world. Furthermore, Aristotle's three conditions of motion pose no problem for the creation of the universe for the simple reason that creation is not a motion.

What Thomas is saying is this. For the world to be created it is not necessary that God precede the world in time. Rather, He must precede it in power. A thing is created to the extent that it depends for its being on another. Hence even if the world had no beginning in the past, it would still be created because it depends for its existence on God.

Thus St. Thomas holds that neither extreme can demonstrate its case. At best, one can only establish that the world in its present state was preceded by the world in some radically different state. From the nature of the material world one cannot establish one way or another the exact length of its duration in the past. In other words, St. Thomas accepts, as a matter of religious Faith that the world is created in time. From the standpoint of philosophical demonstration, however, he thinks that the case is beyond establishment for either side. Yet whether or not one believes the world to be created in time or perpetually existent, the world is, nonetheless, for him, created.[9]

43

CHAPTER IV

THE THOMISTIC TRANSFORMATION

While St. Thomas inherited a number of views and
problems from Aristotle, the ones we covered in the last
chapter appear to us to be the most important ones to know
for someone just coming to understand St. Thomas. The
reason for this is that the points we discussed give one
a working knowledge of some of the principles Thomas often
employs, and, at the same time, they show a fundamental
difference in intellectual environment between St. Thomas
and Aristotle. It is this latter fundamental difference we
wish to discuss now.

One often hears teachers of philosophy speak of the
"Thomistic synthesis" of Aristotle and Catholicism. The
impression one might get from the way such teachers speak
is that St. Thomas was an Aristotelian philosopher who was
trying to accommodate his philosophy and his theology in
such a way as not to corrupt his philosophy. Such an
impression would be extremely misleading.[1] Once again,
St. Thomas was primarily a theologian. Not only that, to
speak of him as an Aristotelian philosopher is, also, we
believe, somewhat misleading. Strictly speaking, we
would have to say that Thomas was not an Aristotelian,
and that the notion of Thomistic synthesis of Aristotle and
Catholicism is too vague. One would more accurately
describe the situation as a Thomistic "transformation" of
Aristotle by virtue of Thomas's Christianity.

Why do we say that St. Thomas was not, strictly
speaking, an Aristotelian? and why do we question a
Thomistic synthesis of Aristotle and Catholicism? To
take up the first point, we say that Thomas was not,
strictly speaking, an Aristotelian for the simple reason
that the metaphysical principles of St. Thomas are radically

different from those of Aristotle. While St. Thomas uses
Aristotle's jargon, while he adopts from him a great deal
of his methodology, and inherits from him a number of
problems and basic attitudes about the way they should be
broached and solved, nonetheless, on the fundamental
level of metaphysical insight, St. Thomas more precisely
stands Aristotle on his head than follows him.

This is an important point; it is not one that should
be taken lightly. The point we are making is this. No
disciple exactly models his doctrine after his mentor.
Yet in varying degrees one can still be called a Platonist,
an Aristotelian, a Kantian, etc. Why? We would contend,
and we think St. Thomas would agree, this is because the
disciple is in fundamental agreement with his mentor's
view of "being."[2] Certainly, for St. Thomas, metaphysics
is philosophy in its purest form. It is __first__ philosophy;
the divine science.[3] It is that which gives unity to,
and creates the background for, understanding Thomas's views
on man, ethics, God, etc. Thomas himself, then, could not
consider himself to be the simple discipline of some philosopher with whom he radically disagreed on the metaphysical
from Aristotle's. How, then, can we, without serious
qualification, refer to Thomas as an Aristotelian?

This is not to say, however, that St. Thomas does
not in many ways follow Aristotle. We have already admitted he does. Still, it is precisely because of the conflict
between the respect Thomas felt for the greatness of
Aristotle's intellect and the difference he recognized in
their metaphysical insights that St. Thomas went out of his
way to bend Aristotle's mind in a Christian direction.
In other words, at those places in Aristotle's writing
where St. Thomas considers Aristotle's approach to be in
error, St. Thomas seems in his own mind to attribute this
to Aristotle's lack of Christian inspiration. So, at these
points, rather than tear Aristotle apart, St. Thomas tries
to inject into and, then educe from, Aristotle's doctrine
as much of Thomas's correction as the framework of
Aristotle can hold.

If the situation is, by and large, the way we describe
it, why do many teachers of philosophy put emphasis on
a "synthesis" of Aristotle and Thomas rather than on a

Thomistic "transformation" of Aristotle? This is difficult
to say, but perhaps we can suggest a few reasons for such
an interpretation. First of all, the metaphysics of
both Aristotle and Thomas is difficult to understand.
Since the doctrine of each man is complex and, at times,
confusing, and since Thomas uses much the same vocabulary
to express his own doctrine as Aristotle did to express his,
one could, if one were not extremely careful, think they
were saying much the same thing. Second, even many of
Thomas's most faithful modern followers have, at times,
misrepresented Thomas's basic metaphysical insight. For
instance, as keen a thinker as Etienne Gilson, perhaps
the leading Thomistic scholar of the twentieth century,
could write in a work called The Philosopher and Theology:

> Some of us remember reading and teaching
> the doctrine of St. Thomas for years with-
> out realizing the true meaning of its
> notion of being, on which, in philosophy,
> everything else hangs. How long was I
> able to circle round this notion without
> seeing it? Twenty years perhaps. Worse
> still theologians who have deeply pene-
> trated the meaning of the Thomistic notion
> of God have been known to teach and to
> preach the doctrine of Thomas Aquinas with-
> out ever understanding the true meaning of
> the composition of essence and existence in
> finite beings.[4]

Since some of Thomas's best contemporary interpreters
have failed to convey a faithful picture of his metaphysical
views, it is difficult to blame philosophers who do not
specialize in St. Thomas for misunderstanding him. Finally,
historically the transformation of Aristotle's thought
made by St. Thomas was achieved at a time when the medieval
period was just beginning to re-establish formal learning
in continental Europe. It occurred at a time when
Aristotle's writings were just beginning to be re-discovered
by the West, and when Aristotle's own metaphysical position
was not well-known.[5] At such a time one might well not
anticipate a thinker would not only master Aristotle's
teachings, but would, also, express a new metaphysical
doctrine while using essentially the same vocabulary as
Aristotle. Hence many of the immediate disciples of Thomas

treated his doctrine, more or less, as an Aristotelian
philosophy. One might say, then, that Thomas's own
disciples gave his doctrine the reputation of being an
Aristotelian "synthesis."[6] There may be other reasons why
some teachers of philosophy fail to recognize the
uniqueness of Thomas's metaphysical insight.[7] We have
simply tried to show that the cause for their confusion may
not be entirely their fault. Some of the burden must be
borne by historical events and by Thomas's own disciples.

Going Beyond Aristotle

To understand the precise point where St. Thomas
goes beyond Aristotle, it is necessary to recall the point
we made before about the starting point of metaphysical
insight. Human beings come to know in two basic ways:
one immediate and requiring no previous study; and one
mediate and requiring exercise of a complex process of
reasoning, and presupposing some immediate and evident
knowledge. The question is, "What is it that the human
mind grasps in its first act of knowing?" The answer which
most of us would give to such a question would probably be,
"something-which-is." We know there is a "something" that
we know, but just what that something is is not exactly
clear. Yet it is this "something-which-is" which is the
starting point of everything else we ever come to know.
For everything else we know we relate back to what we know
this "something-which-is" to be.

Both St. Thomas and Aristotle would agree with our
thinking here. St. Thomas, for instance, says, at the
beginning of his career as a metaphysician, ". . .the first
conceptions of the intellect are . . .'a being' and 'an essence'";[8] and Aristotle before him says in his own
<u>Metaphysics</u>:

> There is a science which investigates being
> as being and the attributes which belong to
> this in virtue of its own nature. Now this
> is not the same as any of the so-called
> special sciences; for none of these others
> treats universally of being as being. They
> cut off a part of being and investigate the
> attribute of this part; this is what the

the mathematical sciences for instance do. Now since we are seeking the first principles and highest causes, clearly there must be something to which these belong in virtue of its own nature.[9]

The major difference between Aristotle and St. Thomas, however, lies in their understanding of the terms "being" (ens) and essence (essentia). For Aristotle the term "being" has more than one meaning. For example, it can refer to an individual thing or it can refer to what a thing is, that is, to a thing's essence. In addition, for Aristotle a thing's essence consists of a form without matter.[10] For St. Thomas, on the other hand, the term "being" has a more complex meaning. For example, it can refer to an individual thing; or it can mean what a thing is, in which case it refers to the essence of a thing; or it can mean that a thing is, in which case it refers to the fact that a thing is. Furthermore, "St. Thomas's conception of essence is not identical with that of Aristotle." Even though ". . .he benignly interprets Aristotle's doctrine as in accord with his own," he was critical of the doctrine that the whole essence of a species consists of the form alone.[11]

No doubt, by this point some readers will be experiencing a little uneasiness with our discussion here. For one thing, they should be getting a peculiar feeling that all this metaphysical talk, which should appear to them to go against their normal way of understanding, is foreign, if not downright odd. In addition, some may be wondering why anyone could be concerned about such "nonsense" as whether "being" refers to what a thing is or to what a thing is and the fact that it is, or whether "essence" refers to form without matter or to form and matter.

We must admit that, at first sight, the whole enterprise might seem silly, in fact almost necessarily so, to some people. Nevertheless, we are immediately brought back to the fact that all of our knowledge depends on how we understand what makes a thing to be, or to put it in another way, to be real. In addition, when we clear away some of the jargon and get to the heart of the issue, we find the problem to be very serious indeed.

Once again, for Aristotle any and every being of the physical world is composed of two powers--one active and definite, which he called "form," and the other passive and indefinite, called "matter." The most basic and underlying fact of nature for him was that there exist things which undergo alterations or changes; and for this to occur there must be two requisites. First, there must be underlying-subjects, and there must be alterations which can happen to underlying-subjects. What we might in a general way of talking call a "thing" Aristotle called "a being" or "a substance;" and what we call an "alteration," "characteristic" or "feature" Aristotle called an "accident" or "accidental form." Since things not only change by taking on different features, but also by coming to be and passing away (that is, not only do things change features while remaining the same things; they also change as things, one thing becoming another thing), Aristotle holds there must be something definite and distinctive (substantial form) and something indefinite (prime matter) about the thing independently of what can happen to a thing in one way or another (that is, an accidental form).

So, when all is said and done, "to be" for Aristotle means "to be definite," to be in some way or another; and this simply means that "to be," for him, means "to be a form." Since, in turn, every form, for him, is a species, to say that anything "is" is to say that that thing is its species; and since the form of a thing is what we know about the thing, we could never really know a thing as individual. Beyond this, whatever a thing possesses by its form, essence or nature is something that thing can never be without. This is so for the simple reason that the essence of a thing is its distinguishing characteristic. It is that which separates one kind of thing from another kind of thing. Now, if the fact that something exists is possessed by that thing by virtue of its form, essence or nature, existence is something that thing never can be without. Hence everything by nature of its form is eternal.[12] Finally, even if one were to go along with all this, it should be evident to anyone that the mere fact that a thing has a distinguishing characteristic, or is definite in one way or another, is not sufficient explanation for the fact that that thing is.

Obviously, St. Thomas could go along with none of this.

As an ancient Greek it never dawned upon Aristotle to ask the question, "Why is there something rather than nothing?"[13] As a Christian, however, St. Thomas could not avoid the question. The most obvious fact of nature for him was not that a thing is definite, or that a thing changes, but that a thing "is" in the first place. Hence he set about "benignly" restructuring the entire Aristotelian body of learning by reinterpreting Aristotle's two substantial principles of form and matter in light of a third principle which he called the act-of-existing (esse). For Aristotle "to be" means simply "to be a sub-stance," which, in turn, is reduced by him to mean "to be a species." For St. Thomas, on the other hand, "to be" does not mean "to be a substance" or "to be a species." What it means is that a thing possesses an energizing act, or force which is that thing's most basic and dynamic act, namely the act which distinguishes that thing from that which can in no way be actual without it. As St. Thomas puts it, "to be is the actuality of all acts and consequently the perfection of all perfections."[14]

St. Thomas's Understanding of Being (Ens)

Very few of us have a problem understanding that when we talk about something real about something which is, we can be talking about a thing, or sometimes about the feature of a thing. At other times we might be talking about what goes to make up a thing, or about some deficiency in a thing; but, by and large, these are the different ways we talk about something real. St. Thomas realized this. In fact, these are precisely the different ways he says we predicate being (ens), that is, talk about being.

For him the term "being" (ens) refers to a that which is. Thus when speaking about a being, we can be talking about a that which is, or we can be talking about a that which is, or we can be talking about a that which is. That is, we can be talking about the-thing-which-exists, putting an emphasis on the thing as existing; or we can be talking about the thing which exists, putting an emphasis on the thing rather than on its existing; or finally, when talking about being in the first sense, we can be emphasizing some concretely existing thing or aspect of a thing. As

Thomas puts it, when talking about being we are talking about:
1) a substance, 2) the form, matter or act-of-existing of
a substance; 3) an accident of a substance; 4) or some
privation of a substance.[15] Thus for Thomas, being (ens)
signified that-which-has-the-act-of-existing, that is,
". . .an existing thing, endowed with an essence and
exercising the act of existing."[16] At the same time,
being (ens) can signify something which is not real, something, namely, which is produced by the mind when the mind
composes a proposition. That is, we can call "beings" those
mental entities or concepts about which we can make
intelligible statements because the judgment of the intellect
gives them a being of reason (ens rationis), even though they
have no being of nature (ens naturae). It is important to
note that "being" does not refer to the concept as such,
but to the concept as signifiable by an affirmative proposition. In other words, these mental features which have no
being in nature get their status as beings from the judging
operation of the mind. Thus privations and negations,
like blindness and nothing, are called beings in this
second sense, not because they can be conceptualized, but
because the mind can form an affirmative proposition about
them.[17]

    We should be able to see at this point that, for
Thomas, the term "being" signifies primarily a composite
reality. It is for this reason that he distinguishes the
two different kinds of abstraction of the human intellect.
These operations are analogous to the composite structure
of being. The static character of essence is grasped in
a static apprehension of the intellect, the type of
apprehension which dominates, for Thomas, the physical and
mathematical sciences. The dynamic character of the act-
of-existing, on the other hand, is grasped in the act of
judgment. In short, the fact that physical being is
composite in nature demands that the human mind reflect
this in distinct operations.[18]

Thomas's Understanding of
Essence and the Act-of-Existing

    This may be made somewhat clearer if we can explain
the way Thomas looks at essence and the act-of-existing.
The essence of a thing, for him, is primarily the being of

52

a thing as apprehended as a what.[19] It is what is expressed in the concept of a thing. Sometimes he will refer
to essence as the quiddity of a thing because the essence
expresses what (quid) a thing is.[20] At other times, he will
call it by the term "nature" because "nature" refers to
the essence as concretized in a being as the source of its
specific operation.[21] In short, he looks at essence as a
medium, or a conductor, of a force which we have referred
to as the act-of-existing (esse). Essence is that through
which and in which that which is has the act-of-existing
(esse).[22] Thus, for St. Thomas, the essence or form of
a thing is related to a thing's act-of-existing as
matter is related to form. If you recall, we talked above
about matter being the conductor of a force or feature, that
is, of a form; at the same time, we said that there had to
be a certain kind of suitability or compatibility between
matter and form in order for matter to conduct a form. The
matters we apprehend around us are, in a sense, nothing
but varying abilities to conduct certain kinds of features;
and different forms are conducive to being conducted only
by matters conditioned in a certain way. In much the same
way form is related to the act-of-existing.

   The reason, for St. Thomas, that we find so many types
of substance in the universe is because of the varying
ability of forms to receive the act-of-existing. The
different kinds and levels of substantial being result
from the compatibility existing among certain matters, forms,
and acts-of-existing. The term "being" is, for Thomas,
primarily used of substances, and secondarily and with
qualification, of accidents.[23] In addition, substance is,
for him, primarily a being which comes to us in sense
experience. It is not an inert blob. It is an essence
or quiddity existing by itself in virtue of its own act-of-
existing.[24] This may sound confusing, but it really is
not that difficult to understand. For St. Thomas something
is real because it possesses an act-of-existing, that is,
because it, in some way, exists. Certainly there is
nothing odd, difficult, or strange in this. Most of us
would readily agree with him. The problem comes in when
we try to understand the way in which something exists.
Some of the things we consider real are not, properly
speaking, things. They are what we might call "aspects" of
things, "features," etc. Now a feature exists, but only
because it exists in a substance. In other words, Thomas

sees an order of transmission of existence in things. A
substance exists through the medium of its own power. An
accident, however, exists more like a parasite. While it
does, in some way, add some reality to a substance it
does so principally by feeding off the power of the
substance. That is, the act-of-existing is transmitted
in order of power first through the form, then to the matter,
and then to the material accidents. One might say that
within material substances one finds an order of conductivity
by virtue of which existence is found in the varying
aspects and principles of the substance. The point, however, is this. A substance is an essence which has its
act-of-existing through its own power, or conductive
capacity. It does not exist through the power or conductive capacity of another. Nevertheless, there exist
for Thomas varying "powers" by virtue of which the act-of-
existing is transmitted. Some powers more strongly and
perfectly absorb the act-of-existing than do others.

To see what Thomas is getting at let us start with
material substances and examine the way Thomas views their
structure. Matter, for Thomas, is a power to exist in a
certain way. It is a power to receive one form or another.
Form, on the other hand, is a power to exist. The act-of-
existing is what activates a form's power much like
electricity activates the power of a T.V. set, except
that the activation of a form by the act-of-existing is
more radical. Some essences perfectly absorb, or conduct,
their act-of-existing. That is, they are perfect as powers.
As such, they need no help to conduct the act-of-existing.
Such essences Thomas considers to be angelic natures. An
angel for him has a power to exist. Yet it has no power
not to be in itself. The reason for this is that the
angelic power, or form, so completely and perfectly
conducts, receives or absorbs its act-of-existing that its
act-of-existing cannot be dissipated. It holds onto its
act-of-existing firmly and tightly so to speak. Other
essences imperfectly absorb, or conduct, their act-of-
existing. Consequently, they need an alternative power
to assist them in preserving the act-of-existing as it
dissipates. In other words, such natures have a power to
be (form) and a power not to be (matter) in themselves.
As such, these forms exist under determinate dimensions.
That is, they are quantitative, having parts outside of
parts. Consequently, they receive their act-of-existing

not in one instant, but successively and temporally, never at any one instant being all that they can be.[25]

Beyond angelic substances and material substances there is, for Thomas, God, or what Thomas will sometimes refer to as _Ipsum esse_ (the Act-of-Existing Itself). God is set apart from other beings, for Thomas, because in God alone is there an identity of act-of-existing (_esse_) and power of existing (form). That is, in God alone God's power of existing coincides with, is identical with, His act-of-existing. In every being other than God there is a separation between the power to exist and the act-of-existing.[26]

Active and Passive Power

How did Thomas happen upon this astounding way of looking at things? The temporal sequence is something we will probably never know, but if we can get some inkling of the train of thinking Thomas followed, we might better be able to understand him. He helps us along this path at the very beginning of Book Two of his _Summa contra gentiles_ when in starting he says:

> Of no thing whatever can a perfect know-
> ledge be obtained unless its operation is
> known, because the measure and quality of
> a thing's power is judged from the manner
> and type of its operation, and its power,
> in turn, manifests its nature; for a
> thing's natural aptitude for operation fol-
> lows upon its actual possession of a certain
> kind of nature.[27]

What is Thomas saying here? The point he is making is simply that if we examine the way a thing operates we can discover what kind of powers a thing possesses; and if we can discover the kind of powers a thing possesses we can come to understand its nature. In short, a thing's operation is the medium through which we come to understand its nature. For example, by examining what Fido does we discover what powers Fido has, and since powers must be possessed by some subject, Fido's powers help us distinguish his nature from those of other beings.

There are, however, for Thomas two kinds of operation: one which remains in the agent and terminates there, like thinking in humans, and one which passes over into and terminates in something external to the agent, like a product made by a worker.[28]

At the same time, there are two kinds of powers for St. Thomas. One is a power to operate on another. He calls this an "active power." The other is a power to be acted upon by another. This he calls a "passive power."[29] In addition, every passive power has as a complement an active power. For instance, the faculties of seeing and hearing in man are primarily passive powers in the sense that they have to be stimulated by some influence external to them. Once stimulated, however, they terminate in the operations of seeing and hearing.[30]

The important point which Thomas sees in all this is that in composite substances one finds the power to operate to be other than the act in virtue of which the power operates. For instance, sometimes we see, and sometimes we do not see. What does this mean? It means, for Thomas, that we do not possess the act of seeing by virtue of our power to see. How does he know this? By the simple fact that sometimes we see and sometimes we do not see. Wherever, indeed, Thomas finds a thing sometimes doing something and sometimes not doing it, he concludes that the power to operate is other than the act in virtue of which the thing operates. Not only that, the way a thing operates, for him, corresponds to a thing's elemental composition. A being, therefore, which has some kind of passive power distinct from its operation is one whose act-of-existing is not caused by its own power to exist. If it were all the powers of that thing would be fully operative all the time. In other words, for Thomas the way a thing operates results from its power to operate, and its power to operate results from its nature. Composition in its nature results from lack of self-possession. For composition in nature indicates limitation in existence; limitation in existence, however, suggests a lack of identity between one's power to exist and one's act-of-existing; just as composition in operation suggests limitation in power, and limitation in power suggests a lack of identity between one's power to operate and one's operation.[31]

To put this whole thing rather vaguely, but in a language which might be more easily comprehensible, Thomas thinks the main reason things act in a variety of ways is because those things do not exist by virtue of the power of their own natures. If they did so exist, they would be God. For anything which exists by its own power is eternal. Not even angels exist this way for Thomas. They exist <u>through</u> the power of their form, that is, with their power acting as a medium. Anything which is truly eternal perfectly and simultaneously possesses the act-of-existing; and anything of such a nature cannot be composite or limited in any way. Hence St. Thomas says in a very important passage from his <u>On Being and Essence</u>:

> Whatever belongs to a thing is either caused
> by the principles of its nature (as the
> capacity of laughter in man) or comes to
> it from an extrinsic principle (as light
> in the air from the influence of the sun).
> Now being /i.e., <u>esse</u>/ itself cannot be
> caused by the form or quiddity of a thing
> (by 'caused' I mean an efficient cause),
> because that thing would then be its own
> cause and would bring itself into being,
> which is impossible. It follows that every-
> thing whose being is distinct from its nature
> must have being from another. And because
> everything which exists through another is
> reduced to that which exists through itself
> as to its first cause, there must be a
> reality that is the cause of being for all
> other things because it is pure being. If
> this were not so, we would go on to infinity
> in causes, for everything that is not pure
> being has a cause of its being, as has been
> said. It is evident, then, that an intel-
> ligence is form and being, and that it holds
> its being from the first being, which is
> being in all its purity; and this is the
> first cause, or God.[32]

This mode of composition of essence and the act-of-existing which Thomas finds in finite beings has implications regarding the way we think about being. For the mind cannot separate from the concept of a thing anything which is essential to the intelligibility of that concept. It was for this reason that Thomas, parting company with Plato and Aristotle, held that what our concepts of material things express cannot be form alone. Rather, they must express both form and matter because material things have both form and matter. Thus while the concept of Socrates cannot contain the particular flesh and bone of Socrates, it must contain matter, in some way abstracting from its particular aspects. Yet with respect to a thing's act-of-existing there is no need for one to include this in the essence of a thing. For as St. Thomas says, we can know what a phoenix is without knowing whether or not one can exist in reality.[33] Since the act-of-existing comes to the essence of finite things as something distinct from the essence one need not include it in the concept of that thing; and all this is so because there is a distinction in reality between what a thing is and the fact that it is.

Words We Use When Talking About Being

Most of us are aware of the way we can become confused by words, sometimes attributing to a word the wrong meaning, at other times getting part of the meaning but missing another. For pretty much the same reason no doubt St. Thomas was careful to explain how there are different kinds of words, or terms, we use when speaking about being. Hence Thomas gave us an account of three different ways he understood that we use words when talking about reality.

Sometimes we use a word to express one identical concept. For instance, whether we use the word "man" of Plato, of Socrates or of Fred Astaire, what we intend by the word is some feature which is identical in all three. When we use a word in this way, Thomas says we sepak univocally, and the word we use is, thus, sometimes referred to as a "univocal term."

At other times we use a word to express concepts which are not identical at all. For instance, when we talk about the bark of a dog and the bark of a tree, clearly we understand that while the word is the same the features which we intend by the word are diverse. It is for this reason that comedians and politicians, who seem at times to be so similar in other ways, too, often employ such terms. When we use a word in this way, with what we might call a double entendre, St. Thomas says we speak equivocally, and the word we use is, therefore, sometimes referred to as an "equivocal term."

Finally, sometimes we use a word to express concepts which are not identical, but which are not completely diverse either. We might say that such words do not express identical, but rather similar concepts. For they express concepts which are partly the same and partly different. For example, at times we may say that our body is healthy, or that medicine is healthy, or that bread is healthy. Clearly, in each of these cases the word "healthy" refers to a different notion, namely, to the human body, to medicine and to bread. At the same time, we notice that we use the term "healthy" principally of the human body as the principle residence of health, and secondarily of medicine because it restores health, and of bread because it maintains health. Hence the identical word can be used of essentially diverse things because it expresses different relations that these things have to a common feature, but, nonetheless, in a certain order. When we use a word in this way, Thomas says we speak analogously, and the word we use is, consequently, sometimes called an "analogous term."[34]

Here again we see St. Thomas expressing something of major importance for the formulation of a sound metaphysics. To explain what that is let us once again refer to a very common experience we find people share when looking at reality. Very often we see people agreeing or disagreeing with one another over whether things are basically the same or basically different. Women will sometimes complain that "all men are alike." Some people will say that the word "good" refers to something which is always different. Other people will look at freedom as meaning "being different." And young students of philosophy will continually battle over whether being is basically the same or basically different. In fact, the whole history of metaphysics apart from St. Thomas appears to be one continuous battle between those who tend to consider being to be one (usually called "idealists") and those who tend to consider being to be many (usually called "empiricists").

St. Thomas realized that the only way to avoid the general confusion that most of us have when understanding being was by keeping our concepts straight. He recognized, that is, that distinct ways of existing are known by distinct concepts. Yet all those things we call "beings" have something in common--in some way or other they exist. There must then be, he thought, some concept of being distinct from the concepts by which the various ways of being are known, and which, in some way, includes all the various ways in which a thing may be.

No doubt we arrive at this concept by some sort of abstraction, but St. Thomas realized that the sort of abstraction involved could not be the same as that used in our natural attitude when approaching problems like those of natural philosophy and mathematics. For here what we tend to do is to form a general concept by leaving out what differentiates one member of a species from another. That is, we tend to think univocally; but if the term "being" expresses a univocal concept it expresses something which is identically the same in everything. This, however, would mean that whatever is not identically the same in all things is not real. Such a way of looking at things is astounding, but not uncommon. For one can find it in philosophers from Marx to old Parmenides.

An alternative would be to say that the term "being" expresses an equivocal concept. This, however, would mean that the only similarity to be found in things is in the name "being" which we apply to things which share no real similarity whatsoever. For the term "being" expresses features of reality which are in no way similar. As far as we can see, the only way for us to get out of such a metaphysical maze is for us to agree with Thomas that the term "being" expresses an analogous concept, and is achieved by a kind of abstraction unlike the one we are accustomed to in our everyday approach to things. In so doing, we can approach all the different levels of reality as sharing in an order, and we can restore to the universe some of the balance it has presently lost.[35]

Transcendental Characteristics of Being

Once we are able to make this transcendental turn on the level of abstraction, the mind is able to recognize aspects common to all things-which-are. Even things which are essentially diverse do share features in common. There are features we attribute to things which are not enclosed in any one of Aristotle's ten categories. For this reason they are sometimes referred to as transcendental characteristics of being. These are features of reality which can be attributed in some way to any and everything because they are among the aspects of reality we come to know in our first act of knowing. They are part of the building blocks of knowledge. As enumerated by Thomas the transcendentals are seven in number: 1) being; 2) thing; 3) something; 4) one; 5) true; 6) good; 7) beauty.[36]

Most of the time we use the terms "being" and "thing" interchangeably. Yet as we have seen a number of times, the term "being," strictly speaking, extends to aspects of reality we would not call things. For instance, it can refer to the essence of a thing and to a thing's act-of-existing. When calling some feature of reality a "thing," on the other hand, what we are emphasizing, in some positive way, is the essence or nature of a being, rather than the fact that it is. Hence the term "thing" directs our attention to a composite feature within the being, namely, its essence. The remaining five features, on the other hand, direct our attention not simply to the essence of a being but add to the notion of being some additional relation.

The word "something" is a good example of this. Not only does it, like "thing," express the essence of a thing, but it expresses a negative relation of one thing to another. So, by calling a being a "something," in effect we call attention to the fact that a being is not another, or is divided from others.

A similar situation arises when we use the term "one" in a general way of speaking. When we say that a being is "one," or a thing is one in being, we do not mean a thing is numerically one, we mean rather a being is undivided in itself. Our concept of being as one results from adding a negation of division to our concept of being.

In the same way, in our very general way of speaking of things as true, or good or beautiful we add some relation to being, in these cases a relation of conformity rather than negation. Thus the term "good" expresses the relation of being to some kind of appetite, and the words "true" and "beautiful" express some kind of relation to a cognitive power.[37]

We bring this up simply to point out some of the aspects of being we grasp in our first act of knowing. The human mind has, it seems, a vague understanding of each of these from the time it first knows. As we develop our knowledge by study we employ these notions to understand different types of goods, and different types of truths and different ways in which things can be one or beautiful. Since these transcendentals are so fundamental to our knowing, we do not grasp them by means of a usual concept or by means of our most common way of abstracting. It is for this reason that we know them so well but express our understanding of them vaguely. It is for this reason, too, that we often hear people speak of the terms "good," "truth," "beauty and "being" as relative terms. Our mind is at home in the land of univocal concepts. When it is forced into the area of analogy, it works against its habitual way of thinking. Yet one should note how being, when considered from the standpoint of relation, acts as the goal for our most fundamental ways of knowing: The primary object of speculative knowledge is being as rightly known, or truth; the object of practical knowledge, on the other hand, is that which is rightly done, or the good, and the rightly made, or the beautiful. In each case one can see how the notion of being serves a regulative function in the order of knowing. The wisdom of St. Thomas, to a large extent, rests in the clarity with which he understood this.

PART 2

NATURE

OF

MAN

CHAPTER I

MAN AS INCARNATE SPIRIT

St. Thomas's unique approach to metaphysics has
ramifications throughout every area of his doctrine. His
reconstruction of Aristotle's concepts of matter and form
in light of the principle of the act-of-existing (esse)
acted as a guide for Thomas in an entirely new interpretation
of man. To appreciate the departure Thomas was making
from previous thinkers, and to appreciate the depth of his
insight and of his power to assimilate diverse views, one
must have some appreciation for the context in which Thomas
was working. On the one hand, he was surrounded by a
theological tradition which placed emphasis on the sub-
stantiality and immortality of the soul. This tradition
found its historical inspiration in the writings of
St. Augustine and held a natural respect for Plato. On the
other hand, Thomas was confronted by the powerful arguments
of Aristotle which, in viewing the soul as the form of the
body, ". . .seemed to rob the soul of its native glory."[1]
Beyond this, Thomas was faced with the figure of Averroes.
As the major interpreter of Aristotle then available to
the Christian thinkers of the thirteenth century, the
writings of Averroes held a unique power to influence the
way Aristotle was viewed by the Christian West. Yet, for
Averroes, no spiritual substance is united to the individual
person as its form. In addition, Averroes held that a power
of understanding exists, one and the same, for all mankind.
Not only did St. Thomas consider this to be a distortion
of Aristotle, but he also viewed it as destructive of
individual immortality and of individual moral responsibility.

Thomas sees the major difficulty involved in reconciling
the Christian theological tradition with the doctrine of
Aristotle to lie in the fact that a spiritual substance has
an act-of-existing of its own, independent of matter, whereas a physical form has its act-of-existing in matter.[2]
To unite the soul to the body as a form, then, would, it

65

seems, give to a person two acts-of-existing; and if a
person were to have two acts-of-existing how could a person
be one?

Nevertheless, Thomas thinks that careful consideration
of the matter demands that some spiritual substance be the
form of the body. The reason he says this relates back to
the direct relationship Thomas sees between a thing's
operation and its power to operate. The operation of
anything requires a power to operate; and a thing's power
to operate presupposes some sort of actuality or reality
which has the power to operate or to do things. This
actuality or reality Thomas calls "form." As we pointed
out at the beginning of the last chapter of Part 1, every
operation of a thing presupposes a power to perform the
operation. This being so, from a thing's operation one can
determine the powers a thing has; and from a thing's powers
one can determine the actuality, or form, of a thing. Since
human beings engage in operations which depend on the body,
operations like sensing, for example, Thomas thinks human
beings must have powers of operation which depend on the
body; and such powers must issue from some form which, in
its operations, is united to a body. Yet, at the same time,
Thomas thinks human beings engage in another operation,
namely, understanding, which is not dependent on the body.
Consequently, human beings must possess a power and a form
which is not dependent on the body in a most important way,
namely, as the source of the soul's act-of-existing.[3]

Having this glimpse of the overall way Thomas is inclined to resolve the issue, let us pause to consider what
he finds objectionable in Averroes and in Plato on the subject
of human nature. As Thomas understands it, the position of
Averroes is that a man's power of understanding (which
Averroes calls the "possible intellect") exists apart from
any individual, human being. To explain how a particular
man knows, even though his understanding power is separated
from him, Averroes tries to find some **uni**on between <u>a</u> man
and his understanding power. This union Averroes locates in
the thing which is understood rather than in the power of
understanding. He accomplishes this by saying that the
object understood has a twofold existence in two distinct
subjects. One kind of existence, an ideal (or formal or
intelligible) one, is in the power of understanding. The
other kind of existence is a real one which exists in the

human imagination. The only union, then, that the separated power of understanding has with the individual person arises from the supposed fact that the individual person and the power of understanding share in some way an awareness caused by the same object.[4]

St. Thomas objects to Averroes on the following grounds. He says that the union made by Averroes is in no way sufficient to explain how the individual man understands. What constitutes a knower is precisely the possession of some power of understanding which apprehends the characteristics or forms of things, not the fact that one possesses a power different from understanding which apprehends images of characteristics or forms of things. The fact that one possesses a power different than understanding which apprehends images of things no more constitutes one as a knower, says Thomas, than the fact that a wall has color in it constitutes the wall as a seer.[5]

On this issue Thomas finds Plato's response to be better than that of Averroes. For even though Plato does not consider a spiritual substance to be the form of the body, he at least leaves the power of understanding in the thing which understands. Yet Thomas thinks Plato is wrong not to consider a spiritual substance to be the form of the body. Plato had held that the soul is in the body like a sailor is in a ship. There exists between soul and body motor-mobile relationship in the sense that they cooperate in operation. Such a union, for Thomas, is not sufficient. A real unity for him must be a unity in existence rather than a unity in operation. If Plato were right, Thomas thinks animal life would be unnatural for man, and it would be impossible to account for sensation. For sensation, as Thomas understands it, requires the posesssion of a body.[6]

How A Spiritual Substance Can

Be United To A Body

The major weakness Thomas finds in both Plato and Averroes lies in their attempt to consider the union of soul and body to be one of operation rather than one of existence. To rehabilitate their views Thomas interprets the unity of man in light of his own metaphysics. To miss this point is to misunderstand Thomas's position on the nature of man.[7]

To understand Thomas's position one must recall Thomas's five-fold division of the physical world which we spoke of briefly in Chapter III. As Thomas sees it, the diverse classes of things we see around us—elements, composites, plants, animals and man—are related in a hierarchial way. The higher level surpasses the lower by virtue of mainly three things: 1) the intensity of its force; 2) the extension of its freedom; and 3) the width of its sphere of influence. That is, for Thomas, there are different orders of physical forms. Some are more active than others. The reason for this lies in the degree of dependence the form has on matter for the performance of its operation. The more intense a form's force is, the less that form needs matter to conduct it, and the more extensive is its sphere of influence, and the freer it is in its operation.

Thus Thomas considers an element to be the lowest form of physical reality because the kind of activity in which it engages does not extend beyond the influence it exerts on the quality of its body. Of all the kinds of operation this form exerts the least amount on others, manifests the least degree of novelty in its operation, and is most subject to control by its environment.

The second level of physical form, for Thomas, is that of a mineral body, something like a magnet, for instance, which Thomas thinks is able, in a greater degree than an element, to exert an influence on others and to be less subject to control by others. It is able to do this, however, only because of some external influence on it by others, for instance, by planetary movements.

The third level of physical form is that of a vegetative soul. This form exerts an influence on the growth and development of its own body, and on the reproduction of other bodies of the same species. Thus its power to influence others is greater and more interior to it than is the power of a mineral or element. In addition, its operation is more multi-dimensional, so to speak. For its operation proceeds in different directions. Finally, it is more in control of its destiny than is the element or the mineral.

The fourth level of physical form is that of an animal soul. This form exerts an influence on the growth, development and sense awareness of a being. In addition, it causes the power of sexual reproduction through which one animal exerts an influence on the growth and development of another animal through, in most cases, union with a third animal.

The most influential of physical forms is the human soul. It has an activity which, Thomas says, does not at all depend on matter, and does not require a corporeal organ as does sensation. This operation is understanding. It is because of the fact that the soul can engage in this operation without the cooperation of matter that Thomas thinks the soul has its act-of-existing independently of matter. Just why he holds the soul can perform such an operation we will go into later. For now we wish simply to point out that Thomas finds union between soul and body possible because the soul is the lowest of all spiritual substances while the human body is the most sophisticated and intricate of all material bodies. The most sophisticated and intricate corporeal matter acts, therefore, as the subject of transition from one level of form to another, partaking in a sense, of two levels of form. As such, the human being occupies a transitional place on the level of nature and is as difficult to classify as are other kinds of beings occupying similar positions on other levels. For example, there are things we have difficulty classifying as non-living or living, or as plant or animal. The reason for this, as Thomas sees it, would appear to be that in relationship to other members of its closest, lower species its bodily development is more sophisticated, and in relationship to other members of its closest, higher species its form is most feeble.[8]

The basic principle under which Thomas works in his divisions of physical nature is that a higher order of form exerts over matter whatever influence a lower level of form does, plus some additional influence.[9] Hence man's rational soul gives to man's body whatever the sentient soul gives to brutes and the vegetal soul gives to plants. This, in turn, means that, for Thomas, man does not have three souls but one with three levels of operation ordered to one another in a hierarchical way. Were this not the case the rational soul would differ from the sentient, and no one would be naturally rational. In addition, Thomas points out the fact that when the operation of one power is intense, that of another is impeded, and that when one is impeded another becomes more intense. What this suggests is that all the powers are rooted in a common reality or form.[10]

Immateriality and Understanding

Why does Thomas hold that the soul's operation of understanding can be performed independently of matter? There appear to be several reasons he held this position. The strongest reason, however, seems to be Thomas's conviction that a thing is capable of receiving other forms, or characteristics, only to the extent that it lacks the characteristic it can receive. Now the proper object of the power of understanding is the forms of <u>all sensible</u> things. This means that the understanding must be deprived of any sensible form or feature, and this means that the understanding must perform an operation independently of a bodily organ. Yet this, in turn, means that the intellect has its act-of-existing free from dependence on the body for only forms with independent operations have independent acts-of-existing.

To put it in another way, what St. Thomas is saying is this. The object of human knowledge is <u>all</u> sensible features, not just one; but a bodily organ is restricted to the apprehension of a small number of distinct sensible features. No bodily organ, then, can serve as the instrument for the comprehension of <u>all</u> sensible features. By sight, for example, we apprehend color and shape, but not sound, or odor, etc. In addition, the very impartiality of knowledge demands that human understanding function independently of any bodily organ. To show this let us make an analogy. Suppose, for instance, that in our act of seeing our minds became individually colored physically by the color we apprehended. This would mean that in no act of apprehending after our first apprehension of color as a child could we see with impartiality. This would be so because our mind would apprehend other colors through the color of the first, etc., and would, thus, look at the world like someone wearing a series of different colored sun-glasses. For one must recall the mind is being individually colored physically by what it perceives. Yet the same would be true if the understanding were individually altered physically by what it apprehended. So, it appears it is Thomas's observation that the act of knowing involves freedom from the limiting perspectives imposed by the physical reception of particular sensible features which lies at the source of his conviction that the soul's act of understanding can be performed independently of the body.

The Immortality of the Soul

and Personal Unity

Given the principle that everything operates according to its power, and given the fact that man's understanding operates independently of matter, Thomas concludes that the human soul possesses its act-of-existing through a power all its own. For this reason Thomas considers the human soul to be immortal.[11]

What Thomas says here might appear to some to be simply a rehabilitation of Plato's older view that man has his act-of-existing by his soul and that the soul and body share in common only a unity of operation. That is not Thomas's position, however. What he is saying is this. In order for something to exist as a substance that thing must possess its own act-of-existing and that thing must be complete as a power or nature. In a person neither the soul nor the body is complete. Man's soul is subsistent, in the sense that a person possesses his act-of-existing through his soul. In other words, a human person is a composite substance (having united within itself a soul and body). In the person the soul conducts or transmits the act-of-existing to the body. The body does not transmit the act-of-existing to the soul. That is the point. For this reason the body depends on the soul for its existence as a living body, but the soul does not depend on the body for its existence as a soul. A person, however, depends for his existence on the unified possession through soul and body of his act-of-existing. To put it another way, Socrates is not his soul, nor is Socrates his body. Socrates is a unified being possessing within himself the complementary powers called soul and body. Socrates, as a person, has one act-of-existing which he holds through his soul and his body, but which comes to his body through the medium of his soul. As a person Socrates is complete in his existence. As a soul he is not. His soul is united to his body to give him personal life so that the body can provide him with the instruments necessary for him to live a complete life. That is, "the intellectual soul must become the form of the body in one act-of-existence from which will be derived all the operations of life from the lowest to the highest."[12] The soul is, thus, for Thomas, an <u>incomplete</u> substance. It depends on matter not for its existence as a soul, but for its existence as a <u>complete</u> substance, that is, as a person. Thus when a man dies the soul survives, but the man does not. For a man needs a body to be a man. The soul is not a person; it is part of a person, the part through which existence comes to a man. Man is a whole, but he is not a perfect whole. His characteristic operation is intellectual knowledge; but for there to be intellectual knowledge in man there must be <u>co-operation</u> of soul and body in existence. The soul of man does not lack understanding. However, it lacks that without which it cannot exercise its operation, namely, sensation. For this reason it is not the body which knows, nor the soul, but the person. Thus the one possible union which could exist between soul and body and which could do justice to the complexity of human operations is the one in which the soul animates the body of a person as the principle of personal life, growth and development.[13]

CHAPTER II

DEGREES OF PERSONAL LIFE

Since man occupies a transitional place on the level of
nature, man possesses powers proper to two distinct levels
of reality. To understand what these powers are Thomas
tells us we must look to the object of an operation. For
within every power there is a direction, tendency, or what
we might call an "inclination," towards some definite act.
There are, however, two different kinds of objects of
operations: one in which a form is the starting point and
efficient cause of the operation. To this form there corresponds some receiving, or passive power. Thus, for example,
the form or feature, color, acts as the starting point and
efficient cause of seeing, and there corresponds to the
form, color, a passive power, the faculty of sight. The
other object of operation is a form or feature which acts
not as the starting point and efficient cause of operation,
but as the end point and final cause of operation. Such a
form acts as the point of achievement to which there corresponds an active power reaching out, so to speak, for
fulfillment. Thus a certain height is the end point of
growing, and there corresponds to this certain height an
active power, the faculty of growth. Hence in order to be
able to distinguish the powers of man one must keep an eye
on the feature towards which a power is directed.[1]

Granting all this, how does one know the powers of
man? The easiest way to see how one knows this is, perhaps,
by pointing out that man is a being endowed with organs; and
that these organs respond to distinct stimuli. Each organ
is the seat of a power, and the way we grasp the power
conducted by the organ is by keeping an eye on the stimulus
which activates the power behind the organ.

Not only that, man's organs are related to one another
in a certain manner. Some are organs which function

principally in a way which preserves and promotes biological
life. Others are organs which function principally in a
way which promotes and preserves sense life. The reason
for these different levels of organic life lies, for
Thomas, in the principle we pointed out in the last chapter
that a higher order of form exerts over matter whatever
influence a lower level of form does, plus some additional
influence. Man's soul occupies the highest level of
physical form. As such its relationship to man's body
is multi-dimensional. It works on the body, so to speak,
from different directions. Just as in nature a higher
level of form possesses a greater intensity of force, a
wider extension of freedom, and a broader sphere of influence
than does a lower form, so, in man, the soul exercises its
operation on the body according to multi-dimensional levels
of influence. In other words, the soul manifests different
degrees of influence and extension of freedom on bodily
operations to the extent that the soul is related to the
body in a vegetative, sensitive or rational way. For Thomas,
that is, some operations of man are performed with a bodily
organ, like eating or seeing. Others are performed without
bodily organ, like understanding or willing.[2] Of these
operations performed with a bodily organ the least subject
to deliberative control by man are the vegetative ones.
Biological operations like nutrition and growth are spontaneous. The power from which they proceed is less subject
to control by man's choice than is the power to see or the
power to hear. There is, then, for Thomas, in the person a
scale or order of liberation from bodily influence on the
operations of the soul. The soul's destiny, so to speak, is
most tightly tied up with that of the body on the level of
biological operation, and is most free from bodily influence
on the level of understanding. So, there exists a
transcendent order of freedom within the relationship of
man's soul to his body. Man's operations are ordered most
freely when they are directed by the ordered exercise of
his understanding.[3] For in this way man acts most in accordance with the transcendent direction of his principle
power, his nature.

Vegetative Life

For Thomas the form of a thing directs its operations

74

towards the fulfillment of its needs. For this reason, in man the soul directs the development of those powers and bodily structures which enable man to live most autonomously as a person. On the lowest level the soul exercises a threefold operation on the body. First, it confers existence on the body by means of reproduction. Second, it brings to the body, over a period of time, a due size through an augmentive power, the power of growth. Third, since growth would be impossible without increase in quantity, the soul confers on the body a nutritive power to restore what has been dissipated, to bring it what it needs to attain its natural size, and to produce the material needed for reproduction. For the vegetative power of the soul to be complete, then, the soul must generate the ancillary, and hierarchically ordered, powers of nutrition, growth and reproduction.[4]

In going over this one should note the metaphysical foundations of Thomas's view of man even on this most simple vegetative level. For him the simple operations by which a man, or a plant for that matter, feeds, grows and reproduces are expressions of the desire for identity of existence and essence. Through its operations a thing expresses its own self-identity. Plants hold together their identify in a very rudimentary way through nutrition, growth and re-production. Animals, on the other hand, manifest the same form of self-identity as plants, but in a more sophisticated way. In addition, they reach out for self-identity through sense knowledge. Man surpasses animals in both these ways, plus he knows himself through self-reflection; but he only knows himself partially, and his self-knowledge depends upon his knowledge of external objects. As a temporal being, moreover, he always has part of himself outside of himself. Angels, however, surpass man insofar as they know themselves continually and without the need of external objects, but they do not know themselves perfectly and they depend upon God for their knowledge. In God alone is there found, for Thomas, that perfect self-identity of awareness and being pursued imperfectly by the rest of reality.

Sense Life

The vegetative mode of man's existence is preserved by a multiplicity of powers. The same is true of the sensitive mode of man's existence. To live as a complete substance on the sense level Thomas finds man endowed with distinct sense powers operating through distinct organs. To each of these powers there corresponds a suitable object towards which the power is directed and to which it will respond as to a stimulus.

On the lowest level of sense life one finds the particular sense, which, like the vegetative power of the soul, is subdivided into distinct powers each suited to receive its own corresponding aspect of sense reality. These powers are touch, taste, hearing, smell and sight. As divisions of the particular sense power, these faculties apprehend distinct operations (sensible species) emanating from surrounding objects through their forms. Like the different levels of the vegetative soul and of man's soul in general, these powers are related in a hierarchical way according to their degree of transcendence from material conditions.[5]

Touch occupies the lowest position in the order of particular sense because touch requires material modification on the part of man and material contact between man and sensed object. For instance, when we touch anything we are impressed by it and sense it as hot or cold, wet or dry, etc. When we touch boiling water, for instance, our hand becomes physically hot and physically wet.[6]

On the next level we experience something which does not directly alter us physically but, nontheless, requires some physical modification in us as a condition of sense experience. What we are talking about is the sense of taste. A necessary condition for us to taste the flavor of something is that we salivate, but the moisture on our tongue is not a feature physically transferred to us by the sweetness we taste, like heat and wet are physically transferred to us by boiling water. This moisture is simply a condition needed for us to taste. Thus when we taste what is sweet our tongue need not be made physically sweet, but it must be made moist.[7]

On the level of hearing and smell there is greater freedom because here there is needed neither direct physical contact nor physical modification in the sense organ, in the sense of either physically becoming the feature received

or of undergoing alteration as a condition of sensation.
These powers perceive at a distance physical changes in a
sense object. Thus one can smell the odor of the steak
cooking in the oven, or one can hear the beat of a drum, but
one's nose need not smell like the cooking steak nor
need one's ear sound like the beating drum.[8]

Sight is the highest of the external sense powers, for
Thomas, because it is the power least subject to material
conditions. The features of color and light which operate on
the power of sight do so unaided by accompanying material
modifications either in the subject as a condition for
experience or in the object as a condition for operation.
For these reasons Thomas considers sight to be the most
spiritual of our external sense powers.[9]

The five external sense powers are followed in the
order of sensing by four internal sense faculties. These
are the common sense, imagination, passive intellect (sometimes called cogitative reason, estimative sense, or
particular reason) and recollection.[10]

Once again, the soul generates these powers in order
to live the life of a complete form, and thus to be a
substance in the proper sense. Now to live a completely
human life man must be able to apprehend things not only
when they are present, but even when they are absent. For
human action results from apprehension. Without some
faculties for receiving and retaining the apprehension of
absent things man would never move towards that which absent;
and if that were the case man would never come to know
anything because the knowing operation begins with that
which is absent. Yet just the reverse is true in man.
He is moved most especially to seek that which is absent.
Thus to receive and to retain absent things man possesses
distinct sense powers. To receive sensible features he
possesses the particular sense and the common sense. To
retain and to preserve them he has the imagination, which
is a storehouse for features apprehended through the
particular and common sense. For the apprehension of
features not received through the particular and common
sense man has a passive intellect and for the preservation
of those features apprehended by the passive intellect man
has a memory.[11]

The point Thomas is making in this division of sensitive powers is profoundly intuitive. Much more is involved here for him than a simple division of powers. Once again, what he is saying has a metaphysical foundation. He sees the human soul as an incomplete substance which because of its incompleteness reaches out for that which is suitable to, or agreeable for, its completion as a substance. Thus the person by virtue of his soul and body reaches out in his powers towards that which is suitable or agreeable to his powers as a human being. To become completely human, then, man must reach out to that which is absent, but which can be received and retained. Now if man were to reach out only towards those things which were agreeable to him as apprehended by his particular sense man would not be able to distinguish between sensible features apprehended by distinct powers. Sight, for example, apprehends color, not odor. How, then, would man be able to distinguish between them without some sort of common sense? Beyond that if man were to reach out only towards that which is agreeable to his particular and common sense powers, man would not seek things which he needs to seek nor avoid things he needs to avoid, in order to be complete as a man. Thus man needs a power whereby he can receive and retain features which are not only agreeable to his senses, but also advantageous to man as such. He must, therefore, be able to perceive such features as pleasure and displeasure, utility and non-utility, advantage and disadvantage. None of these is apprehensible by the particular sense, the common sense, or the imagination. Hence the passive intellect and the memory are present in man. The passive intellect to compare individual features as to their pleasure, utility, etc. and the memory, when stimulated to action by the pleasureable or useful, etc., to recall the past by applying itself to individual features.[12]

For Thomas, then, cooperation between the internal and external senses is indispensable for human knowledge. Each external sense takes in a little bit of reality at a time. When you look to your left, for instance, you do not see what is to your right; and when you look to your right what is to your left is outside your visual field. Your eyes actually focus on a very small portion of an object. They move right and left, up and down, and through these movements apprehend different elements of the visual object. What you cannot take in at any single moment you take in successively through the movements of your eyes. In this successive way you apprehend the unity in your visual field. The same is true, in a similar way, for sense knowledge as a whole. What cannot be taken in by one sense power all at once is taken in by many a little bit at a time.

Intellectual Life

When viewed in abstraction from his understanding of human nature, St. Thomas's explanation of man's intellectual life is extremely difficult to understand. When put within the context of his understanding of man as an incomplete intellect, however, the doctrine is a masterpiece of insight and beauty. Every power in man results from the complementarity needed in man's being for man to be complete. By this we mean that, for Thomas, everything possesses that which is suitable to it to exist according to the demands of its nature. Human nature, however, is imperfect as a form. It does not have the power fully to absorb its act-of-existing. Since it is imperfect as an act or form, it is complemented by an imperfect power, that is, matter. Because it is imperfect as a power, matter is divided. As a result, as the form of man operates through man's material power man's operation is divided into a multiplicity of operations. This means that man's appetite for completion as an intellectual substance is, also, divided. In striving for completion man's appetite is divided into vegetative, sensitive and intellectual just as man's powers are divided into vegetative, sensitive and intellectual. So, in seeking what is suitable to man as such man must pursue his completion through those things suitable to his respective powers and appetites.

The question which arises at this point is, what is it which is suitable to man as such? The answer is intellectual life. The problem, as Thomas sees it, is that intellectual life demands awareness, but awareness demands objects of awareness. Man is incomplete as a nature not because he lacks a power of awareness, but because this power has no object on which to work. Unlike angels, which by their very nature possess objects of awareness, man must reach out to objects which activate his power. The only way he is able to do this is with a body. Hence man must either possess a body, which is an organ suitable to the needs of his intellectual life, or man must remain, forever devoid of awareness.[13]

We have already examined how man's vegetative and

sense powers reach out towards those objects suitable or agreeable to them. Man's appetite for what is agreeable to his nature reaches out in different directions towards his body, and, through his body, towards the world. In so doing man's appetite is divided by his powers according to bodily and intellectual needs. Through his vegetative power he seeks what is agreeable to him according to bodily life, that is nutrition, growth and reproduction. Through his sensitive power he seeks that which is agreeable to him according to sense life. In so acting man's appetite for completion is divided according to exterior and interior senses, each pursuing a particular object agreeable to the completion of a particular power. At this point, we must consider how man's intellectual power pursues that object suitable to it.

The answer we seek lies in the awareness that as it reaches out towards its suitable object the intellect operates according to the hierarchical order of freedom within the relationship of man's soul to his body. By this we mean that in the act of understanding man is most free from the influence of material conditions. For the more perfect a form is the more does it surpass corporeal matter in its operations. Hence while the senses are capable of apprehending certain sensible forms intelligible to man, man's intellect is capable, for Thomas, of apprehending all sensible forms intelligible to man.

The question is, however, how is it possible for the intellect to apprehend all sensible forms intelligible to man? In other words, what is it about the sense powers which prevents them from apprehending other than they do? The answer for Thomas is that the sense powers operate through corporeal organs, and are thereby dependent in their knowing on material conditions; but as we pointed out in Chapter II of Part 1, knowledge for Thomas results from separation of forms from their individual material conditions. Plants have no knowledge, for him, for the simple reason that they only receive forms in a material way. On the sense level, man receives forms in a somewhat material, somewhat immaterial way and, therefore, to a certain extent knows. On this level he abstracts from matter the feature he apprehends, but he does not apprehend this feature in a way which is totally free from dependence on material conditions. The reason, then, the intellect is capable of apprehending all sensible forms lies in the power of the intellect to apprehend forms independently of the individuating conditions of matter.[14]

The problem we are faced with now is this: how does man apprehend forms independently of the individuating conditions of matter? That is, what does the operation involve? To put it simply, knowledge consists in the existence of an object in the understanding power, just as sensing involves the existence of an object in the sense power. Yet for the object to be intelligible, as we have seen, knowledge requires that the object be apprehended in an immaterial way. The question is, whence comes the object of intellectual knowledge, and how does the intellect go about apprehending this object in an immaterial way?

The immediate starting point of intellectual knowledge for Thomas is that which results from apprehension on the sense level. To understand this one must see, once again, Thomas considering an aspect of reality within the context of an order or hierarchy. The knowing office of man is, for Thomas, orderly and complex. It is a personal operation demanding the simultaneous and orderly coincidence of man's powers on different orders of reality present in one unified sense datum. In the act of knowing there occurs a simultaneous and hierarchically ordered transmission of the thing known to the hierarchically ordered powers of man.

The way all this occurs is as follows. Some substance through its form emits an operation (sensible species) which acts as the medium or conductor through which the substance is known. This operation activates the particular sense power through the medium of the individual sense organ. Simultaneously, through the medium of the individual sense organ, this operation activates the common sense, and, through the medium of the common sense, the imagination and power of recollection.

In the multi-faceted event of personal knowing the different powers of man reach out, in varying degrees, to aspects of the emitted operation suitable to each power's degree of immateriality. In this way, different aspects of the object are assimilated by the different powers through different aspects of the object's operation.

When one gets to the intellectual level one gets to a level where man needs to surpass the sense powers in his

81

freedom from corporeal matter. The sense powers, once
again, respond through sense organs to an object's
operation. The intellect, however, surpasses corporeal matter in its operations, so it cannot directly respond to an
object's operations through sense organs. The object which
it considers must be considered in abstraction from all the
individuating conditions of matter. This means, however,
that the intellect must raise the thing apprehended beyond
the conditions under which it is apprehended through the
sense organs. The intellectual operation is an operation
in which the body cannot share for the simple reason that
something is intellectual to the extent that it is free
from bodily influence. Hence while the particular sense
can get its object by responding to the immutation of an
operation from some physical thing; and while the common
sense can get its object by responding to an organic
stimulus from the common sense; and while the imagination
can get its object by responding to an organic stimulus
from the common sense, there is no organ possessed by the
intellect which could respond to transmutations from the
imagination. How, then, does the intellect come to know
from the senses and the imagination?

The answer lies for Thomas in what he sees as a twofold
division of the understanding power into active and possible
intellect. The operation emitted from the sense object
(sensible species) causes in the imaginative power an image
(phantasma) of the particular thing. This image is the
effect made by a particular thing's operation as existing in
the sense organs. Through this image, rather than through
a sense organ, man's intellect is able to apprehend the
thing as such. The way this happens is, for Thomas, that
the operation of the thing in the image is considered in
abstraction by one division of the understanding. The active
intellect apprehends the operation of the thing in abstraction
from any and all material conditions. That is, the active
intellect apprehends the nature as such rather than the
nature under particular conditions, which is the way the
nature must be grasped through particular sense organs.[15]
In so doing the active intellect raises the apprehended
feature to a mode of existence free from any and all material
conditions. This feature so raised (intelligible species)
becomes the medium whereby the understanding power, that is,
the possible intellect, knows the thing.[16] From this apprehension of the object abstractly considered there arises,

82

for Thomas, a concept. The concept itself is not, therefore, a mental invention which arises from the deliberative activity of the mind. It is, rather, the spontaneous result of the object known operating on the human understanding. It is the impression left on the understanding power of its union with the thing through a thing's operation (intelligible species).[17]

The impression left on the understanding power results from the existence of the object in the understanding power (sometimes called "intentional" existence). This impression more or less adequately expresses the object apprehended by the intellect. The extent to which this impression adequately expresses the object is apprehended by the intellect in a second operation which expresses the identity or non-identity of concept and object. Since the intellectual power has entered into composition with the object it is capable of understanding whether or not the impression of the object agrees with the object. The way the intellect does this is by now entering into composition with the concept. Then it compares the concept it received by-experiencing-the-object with the concept it received by-experiencing-its-own-concept. The comparison it discovers it expresses in a judgment of conformity or non-conformity of its concept with the existing reality. Such a judgment is called a truth. As such, it is an expression of the extent of conformity between the intellect and the existing reality (adequatio rei et intellectus) and resides principally in man's understanding.[18]

By this time some readers will be experiencing some uneasiness, perhaps a great deal, with our explanation of man's intellectual life. To calm their uneasiness we will try to express Thomas's major points in a more clear and simplified way.

Actually what Thomas is saying is not very unusual. What he is telling us is something we all experience. The problem is he is simply considering this experience in a more precise or technical way. None of us has, for example, any difficulty understanding that we have sense organs. Most of us possess eyes, ears, noses, etc. At the same time, none of us has any problem understanding that we have sense powers. For sometimes we see, hear, smell, etc. and at other times we do not. When we do not, but still can, sense we do not say we have no power to sense. Hence we normally distinguish between the organ of sensation and the power to sense. The validity of the distinction we make here is affirmed by us in another way, too. For sometimes we see people fitted with artificial organs which enable them once again to hear or to see, etc. even though they have been unable to do so for some time because of some defect in a natural organ.

Beyond the mere possession of powers and organs we notice that to sense something our sense powers pick up particular features of sense objects in isolation from individual material conditions. For instance, when we see the color of something we do not see the color insofar as we are physically in the thing where the color is located. The color is in our power of sight and, as such, has been abstracted by our power from the thing. This does not mean that the color disappears from the thing and jumps into us. All it means is that the color is a force which operates on our power of sight. Once again, there is nothing peculiar about looking at perception like this. For Thomas what we experience of the world is _not_ an image of of things, an idea of them, a sense impression, a wave or any of the host of other inventions philosophers throughout the ages have created to account for perception. What we experience is the operation of the thing on our power, and through the operation of the thing we directly apprehend the thing itself. For a thing's operations are nothing but the thing existing in and through its powers. It is for this reason that when asked what we know about something we are ultimately reduced to saying that we know what it _does_ to us. For we know the thing through its action on us. It is for this reason, too, that in speaking we will say, for example, that the sentence, "John throws the ball," means the same as, "John _does_ throw the ball," or as "John is _in the act of_ throwing the ball." In each case what we are saying is that we experience the subject through his action. Well, that is all that St. Thomas is saying. The only problem is that the operations of things are complex; and the powers we possess are multiple.

A second thing each of us is aware of is that each of our external senses picks us an aspect of reality distinctively its own. We do not smell color, we see it; at the same time we do not see flavor, we taste it. For this reason

we would find it unusual if we were to ask someone how his
ice cream tasted and he should respond, "Blue!" How,
then, is it possible for us to compare and contrast
experiences from different sense powers? Sight can contrast
brown and white, not brown and sweet. For St. Thomas the
answer lies in the fact that all of our external sense
powers are rooted in a common power which he calls the
common sense.

Through the individual senses the common sense
perceives a unified operation on the sense power. What the
common sense grasps is impressed upon another power which we
often call our imagination, and these impressions are
retained for us by a third power we call our memory.
Again, Thomas seems to be relating to us something we all
experience. Our experience of something makes an impression
on us. This impression is an image. When the thing is
absent from our field of sense perception, we can still
apprehend it through the impression it made on us. We can
picture it in our minds. Still, we recognize that our
picture of the sense object is further removed from individual physical surroundings than is our sense perception. In
fact, we apprehend it to the degree that we can separate it
from its surroundings.

In addition to what we perceive through our senses and
imagination, we perceive other things. Yet these perceptions
we experience are more involved. They require a kind of
instinctive comparison and judgment. Such perceptions
happen to us all the time. We "feel" something to be harmful
to us or advantageous, we instinctively pursue that which is
useful and so on, and we do so spontaneously, without an
involved reasoning process, by virtue of our particular reasoning faculty; that is, by virtue of our estimative sense.

In each of the cases we have mentioned thus far we have
been dealing with a sense power responding to some organic
stimulus. In the case of intellectual knowledge the story
is different. Most of us are aware of three distinctively
different operations that go on inside us. One operation
is imagination. The other is conceptualization, and the third
is judging. Some readers might wonder why we call conceptualization and imagination "distinctively different." For
they will think that concepts are just mental pictures; but
some serious thought on the matter should make one aware

that when we picture something in our minds the picture we have is more definite than a concept. In fact, there is no one definite picture in our minds to which we directly relate our concept of a man, or of a lion or of anything else. Our pictures or images are less definite than our sense perceptions, but our concepts are less definite than our pictures or images. For example, seeing a particular person, like Sophia Loren, is more definite and detailed than picturing Sophia Loren in the imagination, and thinking about Sophia Loren as a person is less detailed still. The point is that in imagining we abstract from the most particularizing features of something, but not from all particularizing features. In conceptualizing, however, we abstract from all the particularizing features of any member of a species. Yet it is precisely by separating the features of something from their particularizing details that we come to understand. It is precisely because we have a power to do this that we know and plants do not.

There is a problem here, however. How does the mind go about separating features from all their particularizing details? So long as the person is apprehending an object in union with a sense organ one's apprehension will be conditioned by the limitations of the organ. It is for this reason, for example, that Thomas says that the power of sight apprehends color. The power is limited by the organ. To apprehend the features of all sensible things without all their particularizing details Thomas thinks the intellect must, through its active power, isolate the features as such. Once the feature has been isolated it can be understood by the possible intellect.

When the understanding power apprehends its proper feature there is a union in the understanding between the power and the feature. This union makes an impression on the understanding. This impression is a concept. Yet this concept is not a full-fledged awareness on the part of the intellect until the intellect expresses reflection on its union in a judgment. It does this by uniting with its concept and, then, by comparing the impressions it experienced as same or different. In this way it expresses its apprehension of the conformity of its impression with the thing as being suitable or unsuitable, adequate or inadequate. This expression is called "truth."

CHAPTER III

FREEDOM AND RESPONSIBILITY

From the previous examinations we have made of St. Thomas's understanding of philosophy, metaphysics and of man, one cannot help but notice that his thought is dominated by several principles. One is that everything operates according to its power. Another is that an incomplete nature pursues whatever is suitable to its completion. A third is that one order of reality is higher than another to the extent that its power to operate is freed from limiting conditions. Another way of looking at these principles is to say that the underlying insight of St. Thomas rests with his view that the motive force behind the whole of creation is the love of freedom. For Thomas tells us that one is free to the extent that he acts of his own sake rather than for the sake of another. Yet this is precisely what is sought by every incomplete nature.[1]

In the living of his life, man, like every other creation, seeks to exist completely as a man, but this means that man seeks more than everything else to live the distinctively free life of a person. To do this, however, man must pursue that which is suitable to man's perfect freedom of operation as a man; and this means that man must pursue all those things which are suitable to man's individual powers. Not only that, he must pursue them in accordance with the hierarchical order present within his powers.

The Moral Life As The Free Life

People are often confused by just precisely what we mean by the subject of ethics. It should come as no surprise, then, that when it comes to understanding Thomas's

moral doctrine one can come across incredible distortions of
St. Thomas's teaching. It is not peculiar, therefore, to
find philosophers looking at St. Thomas's view of morality
as some kind of semi-prophetic vision of dictatorial
commands derived from the will of the creator. In general,
such misleading interpretations arise, we believe, from a
combination of weak historical knowledge and a lack of
familiarity with St. Thomas. Once someone sees the way
Thomas understands philosophy, metaphysics and the nature
of man, it is easy to see how such a view could in no way
be consistent with his principles.

The moral life for man, as Thomas sees it, is purely and
simply the free life of man, the life of man which is
distinctively human according to the powers of man. Such a
life is, for Thomas, one dominated by love and reason, not
by dead rules and regulations.

To see this let us review for a moment the way man's
soul is related to this body. Man's soul, we noted above
operates on man's body on three different, yet hierarchically
ordered, levels. Each of us has a power to grow, a power
to sense, and a power to understand. How well these powers
are exercised in us varies, but, nevertheless, most of us
would agree we all possess them. Not only that, most of us
would agree that each of these powers operates within
certain definite limits, and that each power has a tendency
to operate in a certain way. Our vegetative power, for
instance, is divided into a number of sub-powers. By one
we tend to grow in an orderly way to a certain height and to
fight off disease. By another we tend to consume objects.
By a third we tend to reproduce. Yet our ability to grow is
limited, as is the order of growth and our power to fight
off disease. At the same time both our ability to consume
and our ability to reproduce are limited to objects of a
certain kind. In addition, each of the above powers is
limited by its organ of operation. Our sense power operates
in the same way. It is divided into a number of internal
and external powers, each with a limited and characteristic
mode of operation towards which it tends. The same can be
said in an analogous way of our intellects.

The point, however, is this. There are certain things
we can do with our powers and certain things we cannot do,
and there are certain things our powers do without any

deliberation on our part. We do not teach ourselves how to grow, or how to consume food. We do not teach our faculty of sight how to apprehend color, or to tend to respond to color rather than to odor. It is because of the spontaneous appetite, or reaching out, on the part of these powers to their suitable objects that we would find it ridiculous if someone were to conduct courses for babies on basic techniques for growing, or for breast-feeding, or for feeling pain. People know how to do all these things according to the spontaneous inclination inherent in their powers.

As we have pointed out several times in other areas, there is something distinctive about the way things operate through their powers. What we are talking about is this. Non-living things are more likely than are living things to have their existence directed and determined by external circumstances. In a sense, the action of living things is freer than that of non-living things--in the sense that the operation of living things more greatly issues from their own powers of operation. In a similar way, animals are less likely to be determined in their operations than are plants because, for one thing, they are not rooted in the ground, and, for another, they are more self-directed, and operate in a greater variety of ways than do plants. The same is true of human beings. They are the least likely of earthly beings to be determined by their environment, or by external compulsion, because not only are they not rooted in the ground like plants, but they make choices not merely by their senses but also by deliberation. In fact, the more one makes choices based upon his own deliberation the freer we tend to view him.

There is something else distinctive about our powers of operation. Every faculty of operation has a tendency, an unconscious drive, so to speak, to operate, and to operate as completely as it can. In addition, every being endowed with powers of operation has a tendency to live as completely as it can by exercising all of its faculties in the most suitable way it can. A plant, for example, has a tendency to live as a plant, not as a rock, and there is an unconscious drive on the part of the plant to stay in existence by exercising all of the powers at its disposal. The same is true of an animal. The animal unconsciously develops certain powers of operation which enable it to live more freely than a plant. By exercising its sense powers in the living of its life the animal is enabled to live more freely, to exert a greater influence on others, and is less likely passively to suffer from the adversities of external circumstances. This is true, however, only to the extent that the animal uses a certain priority in the exercise of its powers. By giving priority to his sense powers over its vegetative powers in the direction of the way it lives its life the animal is less likely passively to suffer from adversity and is more likely to live the complete life suited to its nature. So, not only is there an unconscious drive in all the things we find around us to exist as completely as they can by exercising all the powers at their disposal, but there is also an unconscious drive in all these things to exercise their powers in a certain order; namely--in an order which gives priority in the direction of the way they exist to that power of operation which enables them to exist as completely and freely as they can. With human beings we find beings which are most enabled to live freely, to exert an influence on others, and are less likely to suffer passively from the adversities of external circumstances. This is so because not only are they not rooted in the ground like plants, but also because they make choices not merely by virtue of their senses but also by deliberation. As human beings we unconsciously seek to live as best we can by living in accordance with the most autonomous exercise of our powers. This means that we unconsciously seek not only to stay alive, but to stay alive as human beings, that is, as living, sensing beings, endowed with a power to deliberate. To put it in another way, not only do we seek to live as wisely as we can so as to live as completely as we can; but we also seek to live as deliberatively as we can because we unconsciously recognize that is the way we are most likely to live freely and without adversity.

Natural Law or the Law of Love

We do not believe that the points we have just made will be found by most readers to be wild assertions, or to be far from the way most of us tend to see things behave. Yet the view we have given, in a general and vague way, is just the kind of point Thomas tries to make in his moral doctrine.

90

Thomas's outlook on the moral life of man is often referred to by philosophers as a natural law theory. Recently, however, this way of classifying Thomas's moral thinking has been challenged in Thomistic circles.² The interpretation we are about to give to St. Thomas's moral teaching follows the latter perspective. That is, we do not, in all sincerity, think it is suitable to classify St. Thomas's moral thought as a natural law doctrine. The reader should be aware, then, at the outset, that our presentation of Thomas's moral doctrine is not a standard one. At the same time, we believe, nonetheless, that it is faithful to the teaching of St. Thomas.

Many people are so used to hearing the name of St. Thomas mentioned in relation to the doctrine of natural law that they might be bewildered by our approach. To alleviate some of their anxiety let us begin by recalling a rather simple fact about St. Thomas. That is, he was first and foremost a Christian theologian; one, in addition, greatly influenced by the thinking of St. Augustine and St. Paul.³ What one should expect, then, is that, for him, the measure or standard of human happiness would be, above everything else, Faith in Christ. Consequently, one should also expect that while natural law may play a role in St. Thomas's moral teaching it cannot play the central role.⁴

The point we are making comes out quite clearly, we believe, for anyone who will spend the time to look at what St. Thomas says on the issue in either his Summa contra gentiles or in his Summa theologiae. What one sees quite clearly in these works is that, for St. Thomas, creation is an order, and the nature and the governance of this order is determined by God, who is the first cause of the universe.⁵ Not only does God create everything, but he directs everything back to Him according to its nature and powers. Hence God is that which suitably completes all natures and powers, and every nature and power unconsciously reaches out to Him for its fulfillment. God, then, for Thomas, is the suitable goal of all things and is, for this reason, called the ultimate good.⁶

God, for Thomas, creates the world because of his very goodness. Insofar as He is ultimately good, He freely wishes to share his goodness in a diversity of ways. Hence Thomas says:

. . .since every created substance must fall
short of the perfection of divine goodness,
in order that the likeness of divine goodness
might be more perfectly communicated to
things, it was necessary for there to be a
diversity of things, so that what could not
be perfectly represented by one thing might
be, in more perfect fashion, represented by
a variety of things in different ways. For
instance, when a man sees that his mental
conception cannot be expressed adequately by
one spoken word, he multiplies his words in
various ways, to express his mental conception
through a variety of means. And the eminence
of divine perfection may be observed in this
fact, that perfect goodness which is present
in God in a unified and simple manner cannot
be in creatures except in a diversified manner
and through a plurality of things. Now, things
are differentiated by their possession of different forms from which receive their species.
And thus, the reason for the diversity of things
is derived from this end.

God's goodness gives rise to a diversity of forms, then,
which, for St. Thomas, are likenesses of God, expressions,
so to speak, of the eminence of divine perfection. As
likenesses, however, forms are diversified to the degree
that they more or less closely resemble God. The more
closely they resemble God the more perfect and powerful
they are, and the less closely they resemble God the less
perfect and more feeble they are. Hence St. Thomas says:

This is quite clear to one who observes
the natures of things. He will find, in
fact, if he makes a careful consideration,
that the diversity of things is accomplished by means of gradations. Indeed,
he will find plants above animate bodies,
and above plants irrational animals, and
above these intellectual substances.
And among individuals of the types he
will find a diversity based on the fact
that some are more perfect than others,
inasmuch as the highest members of a
lower genus seem quite close to the next.

higher genus; and the converse is also true;
thus, immovable animals are like plants.
Consequently, Dionysius says 'Divine wisdom
draws together the last members of things
in a first class, with the first members of
things in a second class.' Hence, it is
apparent that the diversity of things requires that not all be equal, but that there
be an order and gradation among things.[8]

Since creation, for Thomas, is an order and since this
order consists in a gradation of forms, it is also necessary
that there by a gradation of powers, of appetites, and of
operations in things. For forms operate through their
powers as driven on by some appetite. Not only that, the
relationship of a form to a material body must be ordered
according to the hierarchical gradation found in the form.
Hence different matters with distinct organic or non-organic
structures must correspond to different forms. This, in
turn, must result in diverse levels of material beings with
different properties and accidents.

The point which comes out most clearly in what Thomas
says is that the order called "creation" is the result of a
rational plan of operation on God's part to express His
perfection in a variety of ways. In addition, one sees that
since, for Thomas, every incomplete substance reaches out
towards completeness through its appetite, and since, for
him, every form is a likeness of God, the ultimate end of
every created being is to be as like to God as possible in
its operations. Seeking to become as like to God in one's
operations is, then, in a very vague and general way of
speaking, what one might call the law of nature for St. Thomas.
This, however, is achieved by man only to the extent that man
knows God. As St. Thomas puts it:

Again, in all agents and movers that
are arranged in an order, the end of the
first agent and mover must be the ultimate
end of all. Thus, the end of the commander
of an army is the end of all who serve as
soldiers under him. Now, of all the parts
of man, the intellect is found to be the
superior mover, for the intellect moves the
appetite, by presenting it with its object;

then the intellectual appetite, that is the
will, moves the sensory appetites, iras-
cible and consupiscible, and that is why
we do not obey concupiscense unless there be
a command from the will; and finally, the
sense appetite, with the advent of consent
from the will, now moves the body. Therefore, the end of the intellect is the end
of all human actions. 'But the end and
good of the intellect are the true'; consequently, the first truth is the ultimate
end. So, the ultimate end of the whole
man, and of all his operations and desires,
is to know the first truth, which is God.[9]

What St. Thomas means in saying this is that man achieves
his completeness as an intellectual substance through the
ordered exercise of his topmost power. This means that the
understanding of God of which he speaks is more like a
contemplative vision of God's essence than some sort of
speculative knowledge of God. This, however, is something
man cannot achieve in this life. Thus St. Thomas adds:

If, then, ultimate human felicity does
not consist in the knowledge of God, whereby
He is known in general by all, or most, men,
by a sort of confused appraisal, and again,
if it does not consist in the knowledge of God
which is known by way of demonstration in
the speculative sciences, nor in the cognition
of God whereby He is known through faith, as
has been shown in the foregoing; and if it is
not possible in this life to reach a higher
knowledge of God so as to know Him through
His essence, or even in such a way that, when
the other separate substances are known, God
might be known through the knowledge of them,
as if from a closer vantage point, as we
showed; and if it is necessary to identify
ultimate felicity with some sort of knowledge
of God, as we proved above; then it is not
possible for man's ultimate felicity to come
in this life.[10]

From what Thomas says, it appears that, for him, man

has a problem with respect to his being able to achieve happiness. For man has an appetite for a goal which he cannot reach by virtue of his own power. To be able to know God, then, God must provide man with a special increase of intellectual power. That is, man's natural power must be elevated to a higher level of intellectual life. For this reason Thomas notes that there is a special way in which divine providence refers to intellectual and rational creatures beyond its meaning for others. Creatures other than man are directed by God to their completion according to a kind of general providence, that is, according to a direction suitable to the members common to a species. Man, too, is subject to this kind of general providence. However, by virtue of his reason man is aware of the governing idea behind God's creation (which Thomas calls Eternal Law), which is the expression of God's perfection. Hence Thomas says that this direction of man's operations as a member of a species takes on the status of law:

> . . .intelligent creatures are ranked under divine Providence the more nobly because they take part in Providence by their own providing for themselves and others. Thus they join in and make their own the Eternal reason through which they have their natural aptitudes for their due activity and purpose. Now this sharing in Eternal Law by intelligent creatures is what we call 'natural law.'[11]

Certainly the fact that intelligent creatures are aware of some kind of order and direction in their powers sets them apart from other creatures. At the same time, for Thomas, the guidance of human conduct of which man is made aware by natural law is insufficient for man to achieve happiness; and the reason for this lies simply in the fact that by natural law man is directed to God not as an individual as such, but as a member of the human species. That is, by natural law God's providence directs men in common, not the individual man. Hence natural law is insufficient for that personal elevation of his intellect needed by man to see God in His essence. Consequently, St. Thomas says in the Summa theologiae:

> The guidance of human conduct required a

95

divine law besides natural law and human
law . . .because law directs men to actions matching what they were made for.
Were they destined to an end not beyond
their natural abilities they would need
no directive of reason over and above
natural law and human law built on it.
Yet they are set towards an eternal happiness out of proportion to their natural
resources, as we have shown, and therefore must needs be directed by a divinely
given law above natural and human law.[12]

To this he adds another short statement a little
further in the same work:

Although through natural law the
Eternal Law is shared in according to the
capacity of human nature, nevertheless
in order to be directed to their ultimate
supernatural end men have to be lifted
up, and through the divine grant of an
additional law which heightens their
sharing in the Eternal Law.[13]

The reason, for Thomas, that natural law is insufficient
to lead man to happiness is because, unlike other bodily
creatures, man is destined for an end beyond his natural
abilities. It is because man is so destined that Thomas
holds man is endowed with reason. So, he says:

. . .God takes care of each nature according
to its capacity; indeed, He created singular
creatures of such kinds that He knew were
suited to achieveing the end under his
governance. Now, only the rational creature
is capable of this direction, whereby his
actions are guided, not only specifically, but
also individually. For he possessed understanding and reason, and consequently he
can grasp in what different ways a thing may
be good or bad, depending on its suitability
for various individuals, times and places.
Therefore, only the rational creature is
directed in his acts by God, individually as

well as specifically.[14]

The individual direction of man in his acts is what Thomas calls "divine law." It ". . .consists of the ten commandments from the Old Testament and the two precepts of charity from the New Testament."[15] In addition, it is, in general, God's way of directing men to cling to Him through love. As Thomas put it in the Summa contra gentiles:

> Since the intention of divine law is
> primarily to this purpose, that man cling
> to God, and since man is best able to cling
> to God through love, it must be that the
> intention of divine law is primarily ordered
> to an act of love.

And to this he adds a little further in the same chapter:

> Again, the end of every law, and above
> all of divine law is to make men good. But
> a man is deemed good from his possession of
> a good will, through which he may put into
> act whatever good there is in him. Now, the
> will is good because it wills a good object,
> and especially the greatest good, which is the
> end. So, the more the will desires such a
> good, the more does a man advance in goodness.
> But a man has more desire of what he wills
> because of love than for what he wills because
> of fear only, for what he loves only from a
> motive of fear is called an object of mixed
> involuntariness. Such is the case of the man
> who wills to throw his merchandise into the
> sea because of fear. Therefore, the love
> of the highest good, namely God, above all
> else makes men good, and is chiefly intended
> in the divine law.[16]

Such being the situation of man, it is clear to St. Thomas that man comes to God through Faith. For the love of God, like the love of anything, starts with some apprehension of the desired nature. In this life, however, we have no apprehension of God's nature. Hence our love of Him must begin with genuine Faith, which, for Thomas, lies in the divine law revealed in the Old Testament and in the two precepts of love of God and neighbor in the New Testament:

> Indeed, just as the origin of bodily
> love lies in the vision accomplished through
> the bodily eye, so also the beginning of
> spiritual love ought to lie in the intel-
> lectual vision of an object of spiritual
> love. Now, we cannot possess the vision of
> God, as an object of spiritual vision, in
> this life except through faith, because it
> exceeds the power of natural reason, and
> particularly because our happiness consists
> in the enjoyment of Him. Therefore, we
> must be led to the right faith by the divine
> law.[17]

From the foregoing analysis, it appears quite clear
that it is inappropriate to refer to St. Thomas's moral
teaching as a natural law doctrine. Indeed, St. Thomas
himself seems to bring in the discussion of natural law in
order to transcend it. What formally distinguishes the
moral life for man, as Thomas sees it, is not adherence to
natural law, but adherence to divine law. Man is made good,
man is made distinctively free as a human person, by clinging
to God through Faith and love. This does not mean that
Thomas thinks man can ignore natural law. Far from it.
All it means is that for man to live as perfectly and freely
as possible adherence to natural law is not enough. It
does not mean natural law can be dispensed with. In fact,
the more strongly one adheres to divine law, the more
perfectly one follows natural law. The natural law reveals
to man things which man needs to know in order for man to
live as best he can as a member of the human species. It
does not give him the knowledge he needs in order for him
to live as best he can as this individual person. This is
something God must reveal to the individual in a personal
way through Faith. It is for this reason that if one
examines the list of principles Thomas sets forth in his
teaching on natural law, it is evident he is listing tenden-
cies of behavior common to all men which are healthy for
all men to follow. These principles, however, are merely
general guidelines. They are not a set of blueprints meant
to cover every conceivable case of human action in its
finest detail. Just as with thinking in a speculative way,
man's practical knowledge has to start somewhere; and where

it starts is with certain principles each of us knows immediately and evidently from our first act of knowing as practical human beings.

If one recalls, when we dealt with the problem of division of speculative philosophy we pointed out the difference between knowing something immediately and knowing by study. The same distinction holds true on the level of practical action, as it does, also, on other levels of human life. Just as on the theoretical level of understanding man's mind instinctively responds to stimuli from a physical reality, and just as on the level of vegetative or sense life man instinctively grows and senses, so on the level of the practical knowledge required for man to live a happy life, there are certain things man instinctively knows. He does not know them by study. Rather, they are the very starting points of the things man learns through the practical living of human life. These are the things Thomas reports to us in his teachings on natural law.

Natural Law

The starting poing for living as a practical human being lies, for Thomas, in the application of reason to the bringing of something into being, that is, in the application of reason to the doing of something. In this respect, the starting point of practical reason and that of speculative reason are parallel. As we saw in our study of metaphysics, the first thing man knows in a speculative way is that-which-is, that is, reality of some sort; and he achieves this knowledge when he makes a judgment as to the existence or non-existence of what he apprehends. The reason for this is that by a spontaneous drive present within his intellectual power man reaches out not merely to apprehend reality, but to apprehend it truly. His knowledge terminates, then, on the speculative level when he understands truly by means of a judgment. In a practical way man, also, spontaneously reaches out to apprehend reality, but he does so in a practical way, that is through the application of his understanding power to the real world. This means, however, that where his knowledge starts and terminates on the practical level differs from where it starts and terminates on the speculative level.

When we think about something, our minds start with something-
which-is and end with a true judgment. When we think about
something-to-do or something-to-make, on the other hand,
our minds start with an object which we consciously want to
bring-into-being, and end with something well-made or well-
done. Hence just as theoretical knowledge consists in
knowing something truly, so practical knowledge consists in
doing or making something well.[18]

Surely there is nothing peculiar or odd about this.
Indeed, is this not precisely the way our minds work, and is
it not precisely the way most of us are certain they work?
Indeed, what Thomas says is so true that we easily recognize
it is only when we know something truly, or do or make
something well that we are satisfied and feel a kind of
personal achievement. We feel this, however, only because
by nature, that is, by an intrinsic inclination or direction
within our minds, we seek to understand truly and to operate
well.

This internal drive on the part of man is the starting
point of practical knowledge, and does not this just make
good sense? Can anyone imagine being able to achieve anything if the starting point of his knowledge were to do
something indifferently or badly? Could anyone of us in all
honesty say that he would expect a person who thought in such
a way would get ahead in life? To drive this point home let
us make several analogies. How many of us would pay our
hard-earned money to pursue an education at a college or
university whose stated goal was for its students to know
falsely? Better still, how many of us would consent to be
operated on by a physician who advertized that he consciously
sought to operate badly? How many of us would leave our
new automobiles to be repaired at a shop which had a sign
emblazioned at its entrance reading, "We seek to do everything wrong"? Or how many of us would buy insurance from
a company which advertized, "You are in indifferent hands
with us"?

From the first principle of practical knowledge, man
is able to apply his knowledge in distinct areas of practical
life. One of these is the area of living as a human being,
that is, ethics. This means that when dealing with the
everyday living of his life man's practical reason directs
him to do whatever practical reason recognizes as being good

for man, that is, suitable for man as a human being.

What, however, is man? As we have already mentioned several times he is, for Thomas, an incomplete intellect. As such, he is endowed with a multiplicity of powers served by appetites. These powers exist in man so that man may achieve completeness in existence. In a corresponding fashion, man's appetites exist so that his powers may achieve completeness in existence. In addition, the powers of man are arranged in a certain order, and this order exists, once again, so that man may achieve completeness in existence, and all this, for Thomas, is good! Consequently, in directing man to pursue that which is suitable for man as a human being, practical reason must direct man to operate in a way which recognizes, respects and conforms to the order of his powers and to the order of appetites corresponding to these powers. In addition, it must direct man to operate in a way which recognizes the subservience of his appetites to the perfection of his powers, and the subservience of his powers and appetites to his existence as a complete human being. Hence in directing man to seek good and avoid evil man's practical reason says this to man, "Seek good and avoid evil in a way which recognizes, respects and conforms your actions to the order of your powers, to the order of your appetites, and to both the subservience of your appetites to the perfection of your powers, and the subservience of your powers and appetites to your existence as a complete human being."

None of this is odd or unusual. Most of us consciously recognize and admit that we have stomachs so that we might live. Few of us would hold we live to have stomachs. In addition, most of us would agree that we have an appetite for food because we have a power to consume food. Few of us would say that we have a power to consume food because we have an appetite for food. The organ exists for the appetite, the appetite for the power, and the power for the life of the person. Indeed, what would happen if we were to try to reverse the order? Here the person would live for the power, the power for the appetite and the appetite for the organ. The end of human life, then would be the full development of one of our organs. This is hardly what most of us would call a "sober" way of looking at things, and it is hardly what one would call a "good" or "suitable" way for a person to live if he were to desire perfection as a person. Yet we do tend at times to look at life this way. We do so, it seems to us, precisely at those times when such a view helps us to cover over the sense of guilt we feel in going against the direction of our natural inclinations. Such pretentiousness, however, is what St. Thomas tries to warn us against if we wish to live a complete and suitable human life. For we have our best shot at living freely and completely by living in accordance with, rather than in opposition to, the direction of our nature. Living in such a way is what Thomas calls living in accordance with reason, which, in turn, for him, means living the life of virtue.[19]

The life which Thomas points out as the good life for man is a life which most of us, we believe, would like to live, but which most of us have trouble living. It is for this reason Thomas thinks we need divine law and Faith. In fact, the way he looks at natural law points out how very undogmatic and reasonable Thomas is. To show this, in closing our treatment of natural law, let us see how Thomas thinks most of us work under natural law:

> All hold that it is true and right that we should act intelligently. From this starting point it is possible to advance the specific conclusion, that goods held in trust are to be restored to their owners. This is true in the majority of cases, yet a case can crop up when to return the deposit would be injurious, and consequently unreasonable, as for instance were it to be required in order to attack one's country. The more you descend into detail the more it appears how the general rule admits of exceptions, so that you have to hedge it with cautions and qualifications. The greater the number of conditions accumulated the greater the number of ways in which the principle is seen to fall short, so that all by itself it cannot tell you whether it be right to return a deposit or not.

> To sum up: as for its common first principles, here natural law is the same for all in requiring a right attitude towards

it as well as recognition. As for particular
specific points, which are like conclusions
drawn from common principles, here also natural
law is the same for most people in their feeling
for and awareness of what is right. Nevertheless in fewer cases either the desire or the
information may be wanting. The desire to do
right may be blocked by particular factors--so
also with physical things that come to be and die
away there are occasional anomalies and failures
due to some obstruction--and the knowledge also
of what is right may be distorted by passion
or bad custom or even by racial proclivity;
for instance, as Julius Caesar narrates, the
Germans did not consider robbery wicked, though
it is expressly against natural law.[20]

Freedom, Grace and Providence

One of the areas of Thomas's thinking which might, at
first sight, pose problems for many people is his notion
that grace perfects nature, that it, in a sense, perfects,
rather than hinders, human freedom. The same is true for
Thomas's conviction that providence is compatible with free
choice. Certainly one can understand why these notions
might appear incompatible. Yet once one understands Thomas's
conception of freedom the difficulty should be alleviated.

A free action, for Thomas, is one which originates
within an agent, and which proceeds from him, in a non-violent
manner. This means that a free action is one which starts
within an agent and conforms with the agent's mode of
operation. For instance, when the eye sees its action is
free to the extent that its operation is _its own_, originating
within its own power, and to the extent that the eye sees in
a manner suitable to the inclination of its power. Hence·
if the seeing were an operation of some other eye's power,
or if the act of seeing were to go contrary to the eye's
inclination, it could not be called free--in the first case
because it is not the eye's own operation, but the operation
of another eye, and, in the second case, because the action
is forced.

What Thomas says about freedom is not difficult to understand, and it appears to conform to the way we generally look at freedom. The free action is non-violent action. It is one which, in this respect, is normal action. That is, it is an action which follows the direction of one's nature and/or power. Most of us, for instance, recognize that as human beings we have an inclination to behave within certain limits, and within these limits we possess certain powers which, also, have inclinations to behave within certain limits. The power of sight is inclined toward the apprehension of color. The vegetative power is inclined toward the maintenance of life. Operations such as these, which originate from our power or nature, and which follow the inclination of our nature or power, are free and non-violent. Such actions are good because they are suitable to the complete and mature development of our nature and power, and such actions are often called "normal" because they do so conform to our principles of operation. It is for this reason that we consider a normal eye to be one which enables us to apprehend color and an abnormal one to be one which is blind, or which through some weakness or other prevents the seeing power from realizing the completeness due it through its power. In other words, the standard which, in general, we use to determine the normalcy of an action is the inclination of a power or nature. A normal action is one which follows the direction of the power, and an abnormal action is one which does the reverse.[21]

Freedom, then, is not something which Thomas sees as proper to man alone. It is something which, in varying degrees, permeates the whole of reality from God to the elements. What distinguishes its presence in things is the extent to which a thing has the power to operate through its own power or nature. There exists in animals, for instance, a freedom of motion similar to the motion one finds in inanimate natural bodies, a kind of spontaneous operation. In man, however, there is freedom of choice. Hence St. Thomas says:

> Among those beings which are moved by
> themselves, the motions of some come from
> a rational judgment; those of others, from
> a natural judgment. Men act and are moved
> by a rational judgment, for they deliberate
> about what is to be done. But all brutes

act and are moved by a natural judgment.
This is evident from the fact that all
brutes of the same species work in the
same way, as all swallows build their
nexts alike. It is also evident from the
fact that they have judgment in regard to
some definite action, but not in regard
to all. Thus bees have skill at making
nothing but honeycombs; and the same is
true of other animals.

It is accordingly apparent to anyone
who considers the matter aright that judgment about what is to be done is attributed
to brute animals in the same way as motion
and action are attributed to inanimate
natural bodies. Just as heavy and light
bodies do not move themselves so as to be
by that fact the cause of their own motion,
so too brutes do not judge about their own
judgment but follow the judgment implanted
in them by God. Thus they are not the
cause of their own decision nor do they have
freedom of choice. But man, judging about
the course of action by the power of reason,
can also judge about his own decision inasmuch as he knows the meaning of an end and
of a means to an end, and the one with
reference to another. Thus he is his own
cause not only in moving but also in
judging. He is therefore endowed with free
choice--that is to say, with a free judgment
about acting or not acting.[22]

Given Thomas's understanding of freedom, it is easy
to see why neither providence nor grace is incompatible with
it. The governance of a provident ruler he tells us,
". . .is ordered either to the attainment, or the increase,
or the preservation of the things governed."[23] In addition
he says that, ". . .it is proper to divine providence to use
things according to their own mode,"[24] and that, ". . .the
mode of acting peculiar to each thing results from its form,
which is the source of its action."[25] In other words, the
goal of providence is the perfection of a thing's power or
nature. As such, the goal of providence is the highest

freedom of the thing governed. Hence God's plan of operation is to bring created being to the completion of its nature by perfecting its power in a way which conforms with its mode of operation. Such a method does no violence to the freedom of the individual. Rather, it increases and perfects it.

In the case of man, a special kind of help is needed for man is destined for a kind of happiness which surpasses his natural powers. Hence by a special kind love God perfects man's intellectual nature. This special love is called grace, and it gives man that faith which makes man suited for elevation to the vision of God's essence by enabling man to cling to God through spiritual love. Consequently, Thomas says:

> But a special mark of divine love is observable in the case of those to whom he offers help so that they may attain a good which surpasses the order of their nature, namely, the perfect enjoyment, not of some created good, but of Himself. So, this help is appropriately called grace, not only because it is given gratis, as we showed, but also because by this man is, through a special prerogative, brought into the good graces of God.[26]

To sum up, the freedom which Thomas attributes to man is not an absolute freedom. Man's freedom is limited by the order and direction of his powers. He is directed by his powers to pursue that which completes him as a nature, that is, his suitable end, or his good. However, man is free to choose the way he pursues this good. He may decide to pursue it or not to pursue it, he may decide to pursue it in one way rather than another. Thus, for Thomas, man pursues his good with human freedom only to the extent that he deliberately chooses to perfect his nature in accordance with the order and direction of his powers, and with the help of sanctifying grace. If he should act otherwise he would act freely but he would not act with that perfect and complete freedom proper to a person. Rather, his freedom would be one mixed with violence and abnormality.

PART 3

GOD

CHAPTER I

THE POSSIBILITY OF PROVING GOD'S EXISTENCE

One of the only features, perhaps _the_ only feature, of St. Thomas's teaching with which most students of philosophy are familiar is Thomas's celebrated "five ways" of demonstrating God's existence in the _Summa theologiae_. The standard method for approaching these ways in philosophy texts is to contrast them with the positions of Hume and Kant. From the standpoint of a healthy exchange of ideas this is all well and good, but the structure of many texts may prompt a reader to think that Hume and Kant are somehow directly responding to Aquinas. Yet when one reads Hume and Kant on the matter, both seem neither to have read Thomas nor to have any direct understanding of the meaning of Thomas's arguments. Indeed, to suggest that they do understand Thomas would, we submit, be misleading.

The problem which most people have with understanding Thomas's approach to the question of proving God's existence, is, as far as we can see, one of presumption. One automatically assumes that one understands the perspective from which Thomas approaches the question. Such assumptions are dangerous and cannot help but mislead. The reason for this is twofold. One is that almost every philosopher uses a jargon all his own. Not to understand that jargon cannot hlep but lead one to misunderstand a philosopher. The other is that Thomas approaches the question of God's existence from the perspective of his own metaphysics. The only way one can fully appreciate and comprehend Thomas's arguments is through an understanding of his grasp of "being," and this is not easy to understand.

For a better understanding of St. Thomas's position on the matter of proving God's existence, let us follow the procedure Thomas himself takes in the <u>Summa</u> and first point out some of the approaches he rejects. One should recall that Thomas lived in an age of intense Faith. The general presumption of the thinkers of his age was not the kind of atheistic or agnostic one that is often found today. Rather, it was just the reverse.[1] The presumption was that God's existence is so evident that no one really could deny it. Indeed, this presumption was so strongly held that St. Anselm in the eleventh century went so far as to encapsulate it in his famous onotological argument. This argument, though it is often presented as a demonstration for the existence of God, was, as far as we see it, not anything of the kind. It was just the reverse. It was an argument designed to show that the existence of God is so evident that it stands in no need of demonstration. Indeed, for Anselm, God exists so <u>truly</u> that it is not possible even to think of God as non-existing, much less to deny it. For Anselm, only a fool could believe he could really think in such a fashion or believe he really could deny God's existence.[2]

This kind of approach was rejected outright by St. Thomas. For him, a feature we attribute to a subject self-evidently belongs to that subject, if, and only if, our understanding of that subject depends for its intelligibility on our understanding of that feature. For instance, when one says that, "Man is an animal," the feature "animal" self-evidently belongs to the subject, "man," because it is impossible to understand the meaning of the term "man" without understanding simultaneously that man is an animal. Such is not the case, however, when we say something like "The man is sitting," because our understanding of what it means to be a "man" does not depend for its intelligibility on our understanding of "sitting." For we can understand what a man is without understanding that a man is sitting.[3]

The problem we have here, as far as Thomas sees it, it this. It may be true that the proposition, "God exists," is self-evident because its subject and predicate cannot be understood independently of one another. This does not mean however, that the statement is <u>so</u> self-evident that it stands in no need of demonstration, or that one has to be a fool because one does not see it. The problem is that there is a difference between a proposition being self-evident in itself and a proposition being self-evident to us.[4] For a statement can be self-evident to someone only if one understands the meaning of the subject and of the feature being attributed to the subject. Thus if someone does not know what it means to be a man, it will not be self-evident to that person that a man is an animal, and the only way one will be able to make it evident to that person will be by some kind of demonstration. What God is, however, is, for Thomas, not self-evident to us. The reason for this is that the proper object of human understanding is the forms of all sensible things. Of such things we can form clear concepts. Of God we cannot. We have only a vague understanding of God innately present in our nature insofar as we incline towards God as that which completes us as a substance. Such a knowledge is more inclinational, or what we might call "instinctive," than it is conceptual.[5] The only way the existence of God, then, can be made evident to us is, for Thomas, through his effects. That is, from the existence of creatures we can somehow argue to the existence of God.[6] This does not mean, however, that we can ever come to experience the self-evidence of God's existence. We can come to comprehend that the proposition, "God exists," is self-evident in itself, but we cannot fully come to comprehend what this means. The reason for this is that our understanding of what God is is achieved in an analogous way from his effects. Thus the way we conceive of God's existence models itself after the manner in which we conceive of the essence of his effects. Our conception of God's essence, then, cannot be separated from the mode of procedure in accordance with which we conceive of the essences of his effects. This means that in conceiving of what God is the human mind does not have to admit that God really exists. For the essence of any created being can be understood apart from an understanding that that being really exists. Now since our understanding of God's nature is taken from our understanding of created nature, we never actually grasp God's nature, and we need not self-evidently understand God really to exist anymore than we need self-evidently to understand that any finite being really exists.[7]

Given the fact that the existence of God is not, and

never can be in this life, self-evident to us, can His existence, nonetheless, in some way be made evident to us? There are those who would deny it. They would claim that the existence of God is something we accept on the basis of Faith alone, and since the propositions of Faith cannot be demonstrated, dealing as they do with things which transcend human understanding, God's existence cannot be demonstrated.[8]

To understand St. Thomas's reply to such people, one must recall what we said in Chapter II of Part 1 on the relationship between theology and philosophy. There we pointed out that, for Thomas, theology contains certain things which are mysterious and may be held only by Faith, and other things which are non-mysterious but difficult to understand. Proof of God's existence is, for St. Thomas, one of the latter.

There is good reason for him to hold this. Faith, for Thomas, whether it be religious Faith or the faith of the person on the street in the ordinary statements of others, is a state of mind one is in with respect to what one understands. As such, it refers to the way we hold onto, so to speak, what we understand. For instance, we say we are "certain" of some statement or that we "know" it, when we understand something in a demonstrative way. In such a way of understanding we accept what we understand without fear of contradiction. In another case, we say we have an "opinion" because we do not think we can demonstrate our case. We might have some arguments to support our position, but we do not think the arguments are so strong as to exclude contradiction. Nonetheless, we take a stand one way or the other. In a third case, we say we are in a state of "confusion" or "doubt" about a statement because our opinion leans in the direction of its not being true, but, once again, we do not think our opinion to be so strong as to exclude contradiction. In the cases of knowing and opining, or what we might call "thinking," we tend to support our position with arguments. With respect to believing something, on the other hand, our motive for accepting what we believe is not the soundness of our arguments but the goodness and knowledge of the individual whose authority we accept. This does not mean we cannot understand the term "belief" or "faith" to mean an opinion, any more than it means we cannot understand "thinking" to refer to knowing or "knowing" to refer to thinking. We speak in these ways all the time. The point is, however, when we are trying to be as precise as possible about the way we primarily use the word, the term "faith" refers to a vicarious way of understanding. It is, in a sense, understanding through the knowledge of another person whom we know to be trustworthy and knowledgeable. Hence the motive for accepting something on faith is the goodness and authority of the individual rather than on the soundness of an argument.[9]

Now the problem we have here is this. When it comes to accepting the existence of God as an article of "Faith," this is possible only to the extent that we are certain that the existence of God is demonstratively possible. For no one can accept as true a statement made on the authority and goodness of a person the existence of whom it is impossible to show. The reason for this is that one cannot accept on faith that which one considers to be impossible to accept, but it is impossible to accept on the basis of his goodness and authority the statements of a person whose existence cannot be known. For if his existence cannot be known, there is no way we can either verify the statements are his or verify his goodness and authority. Consequently, since the existence of God is not self-evident, if God's existence could not be shown in some other way, it would be impossible to believe that the statements asserting that God is come from God, and this would mean that it would be impossible to accept these statements by Faith.

Beyond those who would deny our ability to demonstrate that God exists because God can be known by Faith alone, there are those who would deny any demonstration of God's existence from His effects because God and His effects are in no way alike, there being an infinite distance between them.[10] To these people Thomas says this:

> Resemblance results from sharing a common form, and there are as many sorts of resemblance as there are ways of sharing a form.
> Some things are called alike because they share the same form of the same degree (and such we call not merely alike, but exactly alike). Thus, two equally white things are said to resemble one another in whiteness. And this is the best likeness.

Other things are called alike because
they share a form of the same type, though
to different degrees. Thus, something less
white is said to resemble something more
white. And this is a less perfect likeness.
Thirdly, things are called alike
because they share a form, though not of one
type. An example would be an agent and its
effect, when not in the same genus. For
what a thing does reflects what its active
self is; and, since a thing is active in
virtue of its form, its effect must bear a
likeness to that form. If then agent and
effect are of one species their like forms
will be of the same specific type, as when
man begets man. If, however, the agent is outside the species, the forms will be alike,
but not of the same specific type; thus a
certain likeness exists between the sun and
the things the sun produces, even though such
things do not receive a form of like species
to the sun's. If now there be an agent outside even genus, its effects will bear an
even remoter resemblance to the agent. The
likeness borne will not now be of the same
specific or generic type as the form of the
agent, but will present the sort of analogy
that holds between all things because they
have existence in common. And this is how
things receiving existence from God resemble
him; for precisely as things possessing
existence they resemble the primary and universal source of all existence.[11]

In effect, then, Thomas's reply to such people is this. Even
though creatures do not resemble God according to the way
they exist, they resemble Him to the extent that they do
exist. The resemblance is not an exact resemblance, or a
specific or generic one, but there is a resemblance to the
extent that God's power to confer existence is manifested
in the things to which he does confer existence. Hence
if the existence of something can be shown to be a created
existence, there can be attributed to such a creature's
cause a mode of existing capable of producing such effects
even though we might have no idea what such a mode of

existence in fact is.

Aside from the two positions already mentioned, there
is a third which Thomas rejects. This position holds that
it is impossible to demonstrate that God exists because we
do not know what God is. Yet the key to any demonstration
is an understanding of the nature of the cause. Hence
a demonstration of God's existence is impossible.[12]

The Nature of the Demonstration

In order to understand the method of argument Thomas
employs in his demonstration of God's existence, and to
answer this third objection, one has to have a clear understanding of the type of demonstration Thomas has in mind.
Today, when we talk of a demonstration what we most often
have in mind is the type of demonstration employed in
experimental science, which uses a combination of controlled
experiment, mathematics and some sort of measuring instrument. Such a type of demonstration is not what Thomas has
in mind at all. Yet such a way of demonstrating is only
one way of demonstrating. There is no reason why we should
restrict ourselves to such a demonstration, especially when
the nature of the object does not lend itself to such a
methodology. For instance, demonstrations made by an
historian or an English teacher or a philosopher, for that
matter, differ from those of the experimental scientist.
If there were not some kind of demonstrative knowledge other
than that of the experimental scientist, no one would have
been able to demonstrate anything to anyone else prior to
the discovery of the scientific method around the seven-
teenth century. Not only that, the very argument that all
demonstration must be the same as demonstrations in experimental science is not a controlled experiment. It is a
verbal argument, a philosophical one at that, which cannot
be verified by experimental methods or by mathematics.
As we pointed out in our treatment of metaphysics, all our
learning depends on our understanding of being, and our understanding of being requires a kind of abstraction which is
distinctively different from that of other modes of learning.
This means, however, that the method of demonstration used
by the experimental scientist depends for its validity on a
proper understanding of being and presupposes the method of

demonstration proper to the metaphysician. Now the mode of
demonstration Thomas uses in proving God's existence
is distinctively metaphysical in nature. To criticize it,
then, because it does not pattern itself after the method
of the experimental scientist is ludicrous. This can be
seen, in addition, if one considers that the experimental
scientist is concerned with a different goal than the
philosopher. The experimental scientist wants to know
primarily "how" something occurs. Why it happens is of
secondary importance to him. The philosopher, on the other
hand, wants to know primarily "why" something happens, what
its cause is, and only secondarily how it happens.[13] Thus
an experimental scientist is much like a baker who knows
how to make a cake. He does so by putting in so much of
this and so much of that. Why his cake comes out so well
is of secondary importance to him. If he were to worry
about it, he would probably start to bake poorly and lose
business. This means, then, that the experimental scientist
and the philosopher have different logics, or methodologies
which should not be confused if one wishes to think properly
in each area. The logic of the philosopher is hardly the
proper instrument for answering "how" questions; and the
logic of the experimental scientist is hardly the proper
logic for answering "why" questions.

When Thomas talks about a demonstration, then, Thomas
is talking about a metaphysical demonstration within the
context of a why-logic. Within the why-logic of St. Thomas,
however, there are basically two types of demonstration.
One he calls a demonstration propter quid (because of which)
and the other he calls a demonstration quia (that).[14] While
the difference between the two demonstrations can be somewhat complex, in a vague way a demonstration propter quid
explains why it is that a definite cause needs to be assigned
to explain an occurrence. Such a demonstration points out
that a certain fact is true and explains why it is true.
In so doing, this type of demonstration makes appeal to the
essence of the cause and shows why certain features must
be connected to this essence.[15] At the same time, this
type of demonstration takes place within a strict structure,
called a syllogism. For instance, suppose someone wishes
to know why John is an animal. The starting point of the
demonstration would be the existence of the fact that John
is an animal, and the reasoning process we would use to
explain why John must be an animal would be that every man

116

is an animal and that John is a man. Hence the syllogism
we would come up with would look like this:

> Every man is an animal
> John is a man
> John is an animal

Within this argument the key to our understanding is
John's essence. It is because we know John's distinguishing characteristic, his essence or definition, that we can
argue to the conclusion that John is an animal; and if we
did not know John's essence our argument would fall apart.
Such a mode of reasoning is, therefore, rightly called
propter quid because it tells us not only that a cause for
a feature needs to be assigned, but it tells us the
reason why we must assign a cause with this definite kind
of nature.

When dealing with a demonstration quia, on the other
hand, we do not argue in this manner. The reason for this
is that there are basically two kinds of "why" questions
one can ask. One kind of why-question seeks to know why a
feature needs to follow from the nature of a particular
cause (propter quid), while the other kind of why-question
seeks to know why there needs to be a cause assigned for a
feature (quia). Hence in the propter quid demonstration
given above we explained why being an animal needs to follow
from the fact that John is a man; namely, because every man
is an animal. In a demonstration quia, on the other hand,
one might explain, for instance, why one has to assign some
cause for charred bricks by pointing out to someone that
the nature of the bricks themselves is not sufficient reason
for their being charred. While we may not know, then, what
burned the bricks, at least we know that whatever it may be,
it is not the bricks themselves.

To understand Thomas's "five ways" it is not necessary
for us to understand, in great detail, the nature of
demonstrations quia and demonstrations propter quid. We
only make mention of them here because of the third objection
made in the last section--that the demonstration of God's
existence is impossible because we do not know the nature
of God. It is true that we cannot demonstrate why something is
what it is if we do not know the nature of its cause. It is
not true, however, that we cannot demonstrate that something

117

has a cause even though we do not know its cause's nature.
Indeed, it is for this reason that we know cancer has a
cause, and that that cause is other than cancer, but just
what that cause is, we do not, as yet, know.

CHAPTER II

PROVING GOD'S EXISTENCE

When proving <u>why</u> something is what it is, as we do in
a demonstration <u>propter quid</u>, the central link in our
argument is, as we have said, the essence of the cause. The
central link for proving <u>that</u> something is, as we do in a
demonstration <u>quia,</u> on the other hand, is not the essence of
the cause, but the existence of natures which require a
cause, which we describe by making up some sort of name from
the natures themselves. For instance, when our scientist
who is trying to identify the cause of cancer starts to
look for the cause, he gives the cause a name, and that name
describes an I-don't-know-what-which-can-cause-cancer-but-
is-not-cancer. In other words, the key to his demonstration
is some reality which, because of the kind of reality it
happens to be, needs some explanation other than its own
nature to account for its existence. The central link, in
short, is a something-which-needs-a-cause rather than the
nature of the cause. In a <u>propter quid</u> demonstration, then,
the key to understanding the existence of a certain feature
in something lies in the nature of the cause. In a demonstration <u>quia,</u> on the other hand, just the reverse is true;
the key to understanding that there needs to be a cause lies
in the existence of a certain type of feature in the thing.
It is for this reason that, in starting his demonstration,
Thomas tells us in the following cryptic passage that the
central link to his demonstration is not what God is, but
the feature of the thing from which we derive the name we
are using to describe God:

> When we argue from effect to cause, the
> effect will take the place of a definition of
> the cause in the proof that the cause exists;
> and this especially if the cause is God. For
> when proving anything to exist, the central
> link is not what that thing is (we cannot even

119

ask what it is until we know that it exists)
but rather what we are using the name of the
thing to mean. Now when demonstrating from
effects that God exists, we are able to
start from what the word 'God' means, for,
as we shall see, the names of God are
derived from these effects.[1]

The question we are faced with at this point is this.
What is it about the way things around us exist which
demands that we conclude there is a God? In other words,
what is the central link in Thomas's demonstration for
God's existence? We must ask this question, and we must
be able to answer it if we wish to understand his proof.
Indeed, it is precisely because so many people never stop
to ask themselves this question that they never come to
understand Thomas's argument.

The answer to our question is that the act-of-existing
of sensible things is the central link to his demonstration.[2]
In other words, it is precisely the central metaphysical
intuition of St. Thomas that the existence of sensible
things is other than their essence which lies at the center
of his demonstration of God's existence.

The problem, however, is how does one recognize this
distinction in things? The answer to that is this. The
way a thing operates results from its power to operate, which
in turn, results from its nature. There is no other way,
for St. Thomas, that we can make sense out of the operations
belonging to a thing. Limitation in operation, however,
indicates limitation in nature. For only that which has a
limited nature can have limitation in operations. Limitation
in nature, moreover, means limitation in existence. For
only that which has limitation in existence can have limitation
in nature; but limitation in existence means that one's
existence comes to a thing from a source other than its
nature. For a thing whose existence is identical with its
nature is eternal because it exists by its own power or
essence. That is, its nature is to be. The solution to the
problem, therefore, is this. One recognizes the distinction
between essence and existence wherever one sees things
operating in a limited way, sometimes doing something and
sometimes not. This indicates that they "participate" in
existence rather than possess it by nature.

The general outline Thomas has in his mind as he approaches his demonstration, then, is this. Recognize, first, that, "Whatever belongs to a thing is either caused by the principles of its nature (as the capacity of laughter in man) or comes to it from an extrinsic principle (as light in the air from the influence of the sun)."[3] Second, recognize that whatever a thing sometimes possesses and sometimes does not, that thing does not possess by virtue of its own power or nature. Third, understand that whatever a thing does not possess by virtue of its own power or nature must come from some external source. Otherwise a power could actualize itself, which is absurd. Fourth, recognize that the ultimate source of the feature in question must be able to cause this feature by the principles of its nature. Fifth, identify something in the world of sensible experience which, in one way or another, sometimes does something and sometimes does not. Sixth, from this conclude that the feature in question is not caused by the power or nature of this being. Seventh, recognize that the feature in question must be caused by some external source. Eighth, conclude that the ultimate source of this feature is able to cause this feature by the principles of its nature. Ninth, call this "God."

In each of the following five applications of Thomas's demonstration quia, Thomas will take as his starting point the fifth step we just listed above--that is, he will identify some feature of sense reality which, for him, indicates limitation in existence. To gain a full appreciation for what he is doing in the "five ways," the reader should be aware of the first four steps we listed above for they explain the method behind this approach. At the same time, by paying attention to steps six through nine, the reader should be able to anticipate the direction in which Thomas is going to develop his proof. Hopefully, by means of these suggestions, and by means of a clear explanation of Thomas's arguments, one will be able to understand and to appreciate the strength of Thomas's demonstrations for God's existence.

The First Way--from Motion or Change

The first and most obvious way is based on change. Some things in the world are certainly in process of change: this we plainly see. Now anything in process of change is being changed by something else. This is so because it is characteristic of things in process of change that they do not yet have the perfection towards which they move, though able to have it; whereas it is characteristic of something causing change to have that perfection already. For to cause change is to bring into being what was previously only able to be, and this can only be done by something that already is: thus fire, which is actually hot, causes wood, which is able to be hot, to become actually hot, and in this way causes change in the wood. Now the same thing cannot at the same time be both actually x and potentially x, though it can be actually x and potentially y: the actually hot cannot at the same time be potentially hot, though it can be potentially cold. Consequently, a thing in process of change cannot itself cause that same change; it cannot change itself. Of necessity therefore anything in process of change is being changed by something else. Moreover, this something else, if in process of change, is itself being changed by yet another thing; and this last by another. Now we must stop somewhere, otherwise there will be no first cause of the change, and, as a result, no subsequent causes. For it is only when acted upon by the first cause that the intermediate causes will produce the change: if the hand does not move the stick, the stick will not move anything else. Hence one is bound to arrive at some first cause of change not itself being changed by anything, and this is what everybody understands by God.[4]

St. Thomas's first application of his demonstration of God's existence is, in his own mind, more obvious than the others because it is based upon motion. The reason he

thinks this is, in all probability, because motion is so
familiar to us, and because things which move so easily
manifest incompleteness. Yet while this way may have
been more manifest to St. Thomas, it probably, at first
sight, is not so to most contemporary readers. The reason
for this is that Thomas uses "motion" in a wider sense
than we do. For most of us "motion" means change of place.
For Thomas, as he uses it here, it means change-in-general.
Thus growing taller is just as much a motion as running.
In addition, St. Thomas's understanding of physical change
is conditioned, to some extent, by Aristotle's three
principles of change. Thomas's view of change is more
existential than Aristotle's, but for our purposes in
trying to understand his "first way" it will be helpful,
nonetheless, to recall Aristotle's three conditions of
change. If one may recall, for Aristotle, change entails
1) a subject undergoing the change (matter); 2) a characteristic or feature which the subject can receive (form); and
3) the absence in the said subject of the feature which the
subject can receive (privation). Given these three
principles of change, change itself, for Aristotle, is
simply the transition on the part of the subject from one
feature to another. For Thomas this view is transformed to
mean that motion is that incomplete, in-between manner in
which a subject exists while getting or receiving a feature
it does not yet have.

Keeping these points in mind, let us begin to explain
Thomas's "first way" by listing the essential elements of
the argument. They are:

1) That it is certain and evident from sensation
that some things in the world are changed.

2) That everything which is changed must be
changed by another.

3) That it is impossible to proceed to infinite
in a series where the agents of change are in
essential subordination to one another.

The first element above is important because it
identifies the feature of sense reality which, for Thomas,
indicates limitation in existence. Right at the beginning
then, Thomas had his reader accept the central link to his

demonstration. Once he has his reader admit the fact that some change does occur in reality, this precludes any later shift on the reader's part to a sceptical denial of the reality of change, and it sets him up, so to speak, for the third element listed above which claims, in essence, that the reality of change demands a finite series of co-operating agents.

Once the reader grants Thomas the fact that change is a reality, Thomas has only to prove the second and third elements above. That is, he must show that whatever is changed is changed by another, and he must show that an infinite series of changing beings in essential subordination is impossible. The second element seems rather easy. The third is only somewhat more complex; yet many readers have difficulty with both.

To understand why Thomas thinks that everything which changes must be changed by another, one must consider Thomas's statement within the context of Aristotle's three principles of change: 1) subject or matter; 2) feature or form; and 3) privation. Change, once again, demands that some subject receive a feature or characteristic of which it is deprived but which it can have. It is evident, however, that if a subject is to receive a feature which it does not have it can get this feature only from some being which does have the feature. Likewise, it is evident that if the subject is not devoid of the feature it cannot get the feature (that is, change with respect to the given feature) because it must already have it.

All this being understood, one is led right into Thomas's next point about the impossibility of an infinite series of beings in essential subordination. The type of series Thomas is talking about here is not one of temporal succession. The demonstration has nothing to do with how long the world has existed in the past. In fact, Thomas himself would prefer to assume that the world had no beginning in the past because it is more difficult to argue his point this way! The point, as he sees it, is this--the extent of the world's duration in the past has nothing to do with the causal relations between beings undergoing change in the present. What is essential to any cause/effect relationship is not the temporal relation of succession, but the direct and simultaneous participation of the effect in the supporting effort or activity of the cause.

To make this easier to understand, let us give an
example. Imagine a common kind of change, like turning
on a T.V. set or brushing one's teeth. It seems evident
that the brightness in the T.V. screen has a direct
dependency on the activity of the electricity being conducted through the T.V.'s parts, and that the toothpaste on
one's teeth has a direct dependency on the brushing action
of one's arm. How long the world has existed has nothing
to do with the ability of these operations to be conducted
in the present. They exist _now_ in a causal order, not
because the world has existed for a long time in the past,
but because there exists in the present an agent capable
of producing such an effect in a recipient capable of
receiving such an effect. Hence in response to the question,
"What is causing the brightness in the T.V.?," or to the
question, "Why do you have toothpaste on your teeth?," one
would hardly find this to be a suitable response: "Because
the world has existed for a long time."

It is easy at this point to see how all this is related
to Thomas's understanding of change. To recognize this
one should recall that Thomas has already gotten his
reader to admit that change is real, that it is, or has
occurred. Next, he has shown that the reality of change
demands that a subject undergoing change be changed by some
being. Now he adds an important qualification. The subject
of change is changed by a being which, when it changes the
subject in question, either undergoes some change itself or
it does not. If the causal being does undergo some change
when causing the subject to change, then this causal being
must, in order to exert its active influence on the subject,
have simultaneous help, assistance or co-operation from
some other being. In other words, a change of this kind
would demand the "simultaneous co-operative effort" on the
part of a number of beings to assist in the transmission of
a characteristic to a subject. Yet if a change like this
must be a simultaneous co-operative effort of transmission
on the part of a number of beings, this number could not
be infinite; and the reason for this is simple. These agents
are related to one another as conductors, transmitters, or
powers of operations. They operate only with the help of
another. With such help, they can pass on their own operations to another. Without it they can do nothing; just

like a T.V. set--without electricity it cannot work.

To make this a little clearer let us give an example. Suppose that some change has occurred. Say, for instance, that a large rock has been manually relocated from one place to another. For the rock to have been moved from one place to another, it had to have been pushed by someone or something. Now suppose one person had tried to move the rock, but had failed. Next, suppose that, having failed, he got the bright idea to have one of his friends help him lift it. So, he went to his neighbor's house and asked, "Will you help me move that rock from the backyard to the front?" The friend responded, "Why, of course!, but there's just one little problem. Before I can help you I will have to get an infinite number of other people to help me. So, you go home and wait, and I'll be over as soon as I can." Now given the fact that the rock has been moved, it is obvious that either the man's friend had a change of heart and had invited a few of his friends to help him, or the man had looked elsewhere for help.

The point that Thomas is trying to make in his first argument is simple. So simple, in fact, that it is easy to miss. When something which is changed is changed by an agent which changes in the act of changing another, the agent in question is what might be called an "instrumental" or "conducting" cause. Such a cause can act on another being, but only with the help of a third. Yet this means that a change effected by such an agent must be a co-operative effort in which one cause is simultaneously supported by another, like a sailor is supported by a ship, which is supported by the sea. Such being the case, it seems inconceivable that this kind of causal series could be infinite in nature, and this leads to the conclusion that there must be a first unchanging cause to make change intelligible. Since such a cause is not a motion, but is something-which-can-cause-motion-without-itself-being-moved-by-another, Thomas says this is what everyone understands the name "God" to mean.

A Synopsis of the First Way

Thomas's first argument is not as elaborate as we have

made it, but we felt that Thomas is so misunderstood here that all this was necessary. However, for those who would like Thomas's proof demonstrated a little more succintly and in a more strictly logical form, this is what it would look like:

1) Everything which is changed must be changed by another.

2) Some things in the world are changed.

3) For this to be possible these things must be changed by agents working without the aid of an infinite number of other agents.

4) But all this is possible only if there be an agent which can change other things without itself changing.

5) There must, then, be such a being and this is what everybody understands the name "God" to signify.

The Second Way--from an Ordered Series of Efficient Causes

The second way is based on the nature of causation. In the observable world causes are found to be ordered in series; we never observe, nor ever could, something causing itself, for this would mean it preceded itself, and this is not possible. Such a series of causes must however stop some- where; for in it an earlier member causes an intermediate and the intermediate a last (whether the intermediate be one or many). Now if you eliminate a cause you also elimin- ate its effects, so that you cannot have a last cause, nor an intermediate one, unless you have a first. Given therefore no stop in the series of causes, and hence no first cause, there would be no intermediate causes either, and no last effect, and this would

127

be an open mistake. One is therefore
forced to suppose some first cause, to
which everyone gives the name 'God.'[5]

In the first application of his demonstration quia
Thomas put an emphasis on the thing changed rather than on
the agent producing the change. He did so for a specific
reason, namely because this follows his method of teaching;
that is, to start with what is most evident to the senses
and, then, to get more abstract. As one goes from one
argument to the next, then, Thomas's demonstration
progressively gets more abstract, and penetrates more
deeply into his metaphysical insight that the existence of
finite things is other than their essence. In the "first
way," this can be seen from the way things undergo change.
In the "second way," abstracting from the things changed,
one can see the same thing in the way agents operate on
things.

To see this, let us first list the essential elements
of the argument. They are:

1) That in the sensible world we discover an order
    of efficient causes.

2) That in every order of efficient causes there
    is a hierarchy of causal support in which one
    cause directly depends on another cause in
    order to exist.

3) That it is impossible to proceed to infinity
    in such a hierarchically ordered series of
    causes.

Once again, right at the beginning Thomas has his
reader accept the central link of his argument. In the
sensible world the nature of an efficient cause is such that
causes only operate when they are made operative by other
causes. For instance, in the case of a T.V. set, the set
works because of the electricity going through its tubes.
If the electricity stops, so does the set. In another case,
the rays of the sun cause brightness in the air, or, in a
third case, the falling rain causes streets to get wet. In
such an order the existence of the effect directly depends
here and now on the existence of the cause. The series,

once again, is not a temporal one. In an order of efficient causes Thomas is talking about a being depending for its existence here and now on some other being or beings. He says such an order exists, furthermore, because nothing can cause itself to exist. Either it existence is uncaused or it is caused by another. If it be caused by another, an order of dependency exists between the effect and the cause, and this order of dependency must be comprised of a finite number of beings.

In other words, Thomas sees around us in the physical world things which depend for their existence on other things: the wet street on the rain, the rain on the combination of certain elements, the combination of elements on certain forces, and so on. This order exists here and now and must consist of a finite number of beings. The reason for this is that one cause here and now transmits a supporting force to its effect. Nothing causes itself to exist. Hence if its existence be not uncaused, it must be received from another; but if the being upon whom this first being depends for its existence depends, in a similar manner, on some other being for its existence, this series must be finite or no being in the series could exist at all.

Once again, the reason for this is simple. What we are talking about here is one thing being able to cause something because it is receiving at this instant some _force_ from another. The thing from which it receives this force either possesses this force by its own nature or it gets this force from some other being. The point is that the series of beings from which it is getting this force which it is transmitting must be finite in nature because no force can be transmitted across an infinite medium. Given the fact that the thing _does_ cause something here and now, one knows that this series must be finite in number. This, however, leads to the ineluctable conclusion that there must be a first efficient cause to make the present operations of efficient causes intelligible. Since such a first efficient cause is not caused, but is something-which-can-cause-others-without-itself-being-caused-by-another, Thomas says, everyone gives this being the name "God."

A Synopsis of the Second Way

When examined from the standpoint of a more rigorously logical format, this is what Thomas's argument looks like:

1) In every order of efficient causes there is a hierarchy of causal support in which one cause directly depends on another cause to exist.

2) There exists an order of efficient causes in the sensible world.

3) For this to be possible this order must consist of a finite number of beings.

4) But this is possible only if there be an agent presently existing which can cause other things without itself being caused.

5) There must, then, be such a being and to this being everyone gives the name "God."

The Third Way--from Possibility and Necessity

The third way is based on what need not be and on what must be, and runs as follows. Some of the things we come across can be but need not be, for we find them springing up and dying away, thus sometimes in being and sometimes not. Now everything cannot be like this, for a thing that need not be, once was not; and if everything need not be, once upon a time there was nothing. But if that were true there would be nothing even now, because something that does not exist can only be brought into being by something already existing. So that if nothing was in being nothing could be brought into being, and nothing would be in being now, which contradicts ob-servation. Not everything therefore is the sort of thing that need not be; there has got to be something that must be. Now a

thing that must be, may or may not owe
this necessity to something else. But
just as we must stop somewhere in a
series of causes, so also in a series of
things which must be and owe this to
other things. One is forced therefore to
suppose something which must be, and owes
this to no other thing than itself; indeed it itself is the cause that other
things must be.[6]

In the "third way" Thomas shifts his perspective from
the nature of causal operation to the mode of existing
proper to things around us. The demonstration is somewhat
difficult to understand; but as we go over it, we will try
to make Thomas's position clear.

To begin with, the essential stages of the argument
are as follows:

1) We find around us in reality some things which
   have the power both to exist and not to exist.

2) Whatever has the power both to exist and not
   to exist has its existence caused by a being
   which must exist.

3) It is impossible to proceed to infinity in a
   series of essentially subordinated necessary
   causes.

At the beginning of the argument, Thomas contrasts
the notions of possible and necessary. By "possible" he
means that which has the power both to exist and not to
exist. By "necessary" he means that which cannot not-
exist. It is important to understand this distinction.
For, once again, Thomas begins his demonstration with the
central link of his argument, which, in this case, is that
possible beings exist in reality. What Thomas is referring
to is beings with a material nature. He is drawing a
distinction between the mode of existing proper to physical
beings and the mode of existence proper to angels and to
God. Things which are physical are composed of form,
matter, and the act-of-existing. As such, they have a power
in themselves both to exist and not to exist. Angels,
however, are composed only of form and the act-of-existing.

131

As such, they have no power in themselves not to exist. Their power is only to exist. However, their power to exist is not identical with their act-of-existing. Hence the real necessity by which they must exist is extrinsic to them. For the necessity they have to exist is actual only to the extent that they _do_ exist; but they are only because they receive their existence from another, namely, from God. In God alone is the power to exist identical with His act-of-existing. Hence in God alone does the necessity of existing proceed from the intrinsic principles of His nature.

Knowing all this right from the start Thomas's argument runs like this. He says that we see around us things which have the power both to exist and not to exist. We know they have this power for the same reason we know that some things have the power to see. That is, because sometimes they exist and sometimes they do not exist, just as sometimes one sees and sometimes one does not see. Such beings we call "possible beings." Insofar as they merely have the power to exist, when and if they do exist their act-of-existing must be caused by some force extrinsic to them. This is, likewise, similar to the case of a person who has the power to see. When he does see his power must be activated by some force extrinsic to the power.

Not everything, for Thomas, however, can be merely a possible being. For if all things were only possible beings Thomas thinks there would be nothing in existence at present.

Why does he hold this? Actually his reasoning is quite simple. As he sees it, anyone who denies the existence of God presupposes the infinite duration of the world in the past. As he pointed out in the "second way," nothing can cause itself to exist. Its existence, then, for Thomas, must be caused by another. It cannot be caused by nothing because what does not exist cannot cause anything, and its existence cannot be uncaused because then the thing would be identical with God. Hence when an individual denies God's existence he assumes a temporally infinite series of possible beings existing in the past successively bringing each other into existence, and at some time ceasing to exist. If such be the case, that person, at the same time, must assume that at sometime in the past nothing existed.

Why? Because, as Thomas sees it, something which is possible for everything, over a period of infinite time, must, at some time, be realized.[7] That is, to maintain, on the one hand, that every being which exists is merely a possible thing (that is, is a being which at some time is not), and to maintain on the other hand, that there never was a time during infinite time when everything was not, is to maintain that being merely a possible being is not possible for everything. In other words, to say that something is possible for everything means that, given an infinite time, at some time this possibility will be realized. For to say that something is possible but never did happen nor ever will happen over an infinite time is the same as saying something is impossible. Hence if it be possible that everything can simultaneously not-exist, given an infinite time in the past, at sometime nothing was. This, however, means that nothing now is. For from absolutely nothing nothing could ever come to exist. There is, however, something now. Consequently, there must be something which is necessary. Not only that, there must be something which has its necessity by virtue of its own nature. For a thing can have the power not to exist either because some other being causes this necessity in it, or because it has this power by itself. Now a thing which has the necessity of its existence caused by another exists only if its cause exists. Thus there must exist some being which has the necessity of its existence from itself. This we call "God."

In arguing the way he does, Thomas attempts to bring up the strongest objections he can against his own position. Unfortunately, in the present case this can cause the reader to put too much emphasis on the notion of time in this proof. What one should really concentrate on is not the question of whether, over an infinite time, that which is possible for everything will eventually come to pass. The heart of demonstration lies, for Thomas, within the distinction between possible and necessary beings. A possible being is one whose existence is caused by another. Such a being is one whose power to exist must be activated by some extrinsic force. All the while it exists its existence is supported by another, just as all the while one sees one's power to see is activated by a visible object. If the causes should cease to exist, even for a moment, the effect would cease. Why is it, then, that possible beings, beings which can either exist or not exist, do exist? It is because all the while they do exist their existence is being caused by the supportive operation of some being whose act-of-existing is identical with its power to exist. This distinguishes this being from beings which exist by necessity insofar as they can never cease to exist, but so exist only because they are continually given their existence by an absolutely necessary being.

A Synopsis of the Third Way

At this point we can, once again, review Thomas's argument in a more strictly logical format. When we do so this is the way it proceeds:

1) Whatever has the power both to exist and not exist, when it does exist, has its existence caused by some necessary being.

2) We find actually existing in the world some beings which have the power both to exist and not to exist.

3) These beings must have their existence caused by some necessary being.

4) This necessary being, in turn, must possess its act-of-existing from its own power or from some other necessary being.

5) It is impossible to have an infinite number of necessary beings here and now being supported by each other in a hierarchical way.

6) Consequently, there must be a necessary being which has the necessity of its existence issue from the principles of its own nature, and is the cause of existence and necessity in others. This we call "God."

The Fourth Way--from Diverse

Grades of Existing

The fourth way is based on the gradation observed in things. Some things are found to be more good, more true, more noble, and so on, and other things less. But such comparative terms describe varying degrees of approximation to a superlative; for example things are hotter and hotter the nearer they approach what is hottest. Something therefore is the truest and the best and most noble of things, and hence the most fully in being; for Aristotle says that the truest things are the things most fully in being. Now <u>when many things possess some property in common, the one most fully possessing it causes it in the others: fire</u>, to use Aristotle's example, <u>the hottest of all things, causes all other things to be hot</u>. There is something therefore which causes in all other things their being, their goodness, and whatever other perfection they have. And this we call 'God.'[8]

Of all of Thomas's demonstrations probably the most perplexing for the modern reader is his "fourth way." To understand what he seeks to achieve here it will be best if we first review what he has done thus far. Not only has he showed the dependency of distinct natural events on some mysterious force which he calls "God," but he has progressively expanded the sphere of influence of this God of his. In the "first way" this God causes things to move. In the "second way" He causes efficient causes to operate. In the "third way" He causes the existence of all finite beings. Note that not only does Thomas's demonstration become more abstract as he progresses from one application to the next, but the sphere of God's providence expands. What Thomas is in the process of doing, in effect, is revealing the extent of God's creative power by examining, first, the way the things He causes change; second, the way agents He causes operate; third, the way things He causes are able to exist; fourth, the diverse degrees of perfections in existence of things He causes; and fifth, the

direction of the whole of creation back to its creator.
In other words, not only in each way taken by itself is
Thomas giving a demonstration of the existence of that
being Thomas calls "God," but within the "five ways" taken
as a whole he is effecting a veritable artistic achievement.
What Thomas is seeking to do here is not merely to prove
God's existence. It seems quite clear he is following a
definite order of learning intended to lead the reader to a
reverence and admiration of God's power. That is, by
examining God's effects, Thomas is trying to make known,
and, in a negative way he is trying to reveal, the sublimity
of God's nature. For, as he sees it, we come to understand
operations from things, and powers from operations and
natures from powers. Thus Thomas says in the Summa contra
gentiles:

> . . .this consideration of God's works leads
> to admiration of God's sublime power, and
> consequently inspires in men's hearts
> reverence for God. For the power of the
> worker is necessarily understood to transcend
> the things made.[9]

It is appropriate, then, that the "fourth way" should
not only prove God's existence but should also manifest to
a greater extent than the preceding ways the power of God.
It will do this by considering aspects of things which
involve not their powers or operations, but those transcendental perfections common to the whole of reality. Not
only, then, will we understand God to be the cause of
motion, of efficient causality, and of existence. The
"fourth way" will show Him to be the cause of every perfection found throughout the whole of reality.

As Thomas sees it, a thing is perfect to the extent
that it possesses the act-of-existing. The way things
hold on to existence, then, indicates the degree of perfection they have. When indicating perfection in things
by speaking we employ terms which indicate transcendental
characteristics of being. The more perfectly a thing
possesses the act-of-existing, the more, in an analogous
way, we can call that thing "good," "true," "beautiful,"
and so on. For these terms, in one way or another, indicate
that something is complete, that it possesses what it is
supposed to have according to its nature; in short, that it

is, in some way or other, perfect.

For Thomas we use these terms because we observe in physical things a gradation of perfection. The natures of things are diverse representations of God's perfection. As we have already noted in Chapter III of Part 3, there is a hierarchical order of perfection throughout the whole of creation. The diversity of things requires that not all be equal. As Thomas says elsewhere in the Summa theologiae:

> . . . all members of a genus share one essence or nature, that of the genus stating what they are. As existents, however, they differ, for a horse's existence is not a man's, and this man's existence is not that man's. So that when something belongs to a genus, its nature, or what it is, must differ from its existence.[10]

The point that Thomas is trying to make, then, is this. For the same nature to be communicated to distinct individuals, no one individual's act-of-existing can be identical with its nature. For that would mean that that individual would be its genus. For instance, if Fido's act-of-existing were identical with his genus, "animal," any being which happened to be an animal would have to be Fido. This would be so because a genus expresses something common to all its members. If there is no difference between Fido's existence and Fido's genus, then Fido's existence is something possessed in common by all the members of Fido's genus.[11]

However, just the reverse is the case. What we observe in reality is diversity in existence. We see things existing in a way which more or less closely realizes the perfection proper to them as things possessing a common nature. Hence in his "fourth way" Thomas's argument revolves around the following elements:

1) That we observe a gradation in things based upon the degree in which things more or less completely, thoroughly, or perfectly possess existence (that is, are good, true, noble, and so on).

2) Any property shared in varying degrees by all the

members of a genus is caused in the other members by the member most perfectly possessing the property.

3) There must be a being which perfectly possesses the act-of-existing and all other attending perfections.

The key to understanding this "fourth way" lies, we believe, in one's understanding that gradation indicates something imperfectly possessed. There are degrees of something because no one degree which possesses that thing so perfectly possesses it that no other degree can have some of it. That is, where degrees of greater and less intensity of possession are found, there also is found a kind of conductivity. Thus things which are more or less hot are more or less hot because of their ability to conduct heat. The limited manner in which they possess heat arises from their limited ability to conduct it, and not from any limitation in the nature of heat itself. In addition, that which most perfectly holds on to the commonly conducted feature is the ultimate cause for its being able to appear in varying degrees in other things. Now since existence and the transcendental perfections which go along with it are possessed in varying degrees throughout the whole of reality, there must be some absolutely perfect being which is the cause of existence and other perfections in things. This we call "God."

A Synopsis of the Fourth Way

To summarize, this is the way the "fourth way" looks when expressed in a more strictly logical fashion:

1) When any property exists in varying degrees within the members of a genus, there must be a maximum in that genus most perfectly possessing that property, and ultimately explaining its existence in varying degrees within the others.

2) We see around us in the world some beings which in varying degrees possess existence and other perfections.

138

3) There must then be some being which most
   perfectly possesses existence and these other
   perfections. This we call "God."

   The Fifth Way--from the Order

   Within Natural Operations

      The fifth way is based on the guided-
ness of nature. An orderedness of actions
to an end is observed in all bodies obeying
natural laws, even when they lack awareness.
For their behaviour hardly ever varies, and
will practically always turn out well; which
shows that they truly tend to a goal, and do
not merely hit it by accident. Nothing
however that lacks awareness tends to a
goal, except under the direction of someone
with awareness and with understanding; the arrow,
for example, requires an archer. Everything
in nature, therefore, is directed to its
goal by someone with understanding, and this
we call 'God.'[12]

Thomas's "fifth way" is taken from the orderliness he
observes within the operation of physical realities which
possess no decision-making faculty. They tend to operate
in a uniform direction, and in a manner most often suitable
for their well-being. For example, eyes respond to light,
animal bodies fight off disease, people grow in a uniform
way, and so on. Yet none of this results from some decision-
making process on the part of the natures involved, and is,
nonetheless, most often for their benefit. For such natures
to behave with this kind of uniformity of direction and self-
benefit one must posit the existence of a directing agent
endowed with understanding. For nothing which lacks a
decision-making process can direct its operations with
orderliness and consistent self-benefit. Hence there must
exist some agent endowed with understanding which directs
in a providential way the operations of non-cognitive
natures.

A Synopsis of the Fifth Way

Thomas's argument in the "fifth way" seems to us to be simple to follow. Hence we need not present any elaborate discussion of it. In essence, his argument looks like this:

1) No nature devoid of a decision-making faculty can operate in a uniform direction and in a manner which most often benefits it unless its operation is being guided by a being with understanding.

2) We find around us in the world natures without decision-making faculties behaving with uniformity of direction in a manner which most often benefits them.

3) There must exist a being endowed with understanding which is guiding the operations of these natures. This we call "God."

Some Final Objections

Within the context of his article dealing with the demonstration of God's existence, Thomas takes up two final objections to his position. Since these objections are often made to preclude the case for God's existence, we think it will be helpful to explain how Thomas responds to them. The first objection states that if God exists there could be no evil in the world, for God is infinite good.[13] The second objection claims that the world is a self-explaining fact. That is, everything which happens in the world can be fully explained either by physical causes or man's intellect and will.[14] Thus there is simply no need to suppose that God exists.

Thomas's responses to both objections are brief and to the point, yet his answer to the first, it appears to us, stands in need of further elucidation on our part if it is to be understood by a modern reader.

Creation, for Thomas, is an order. That is, it consists of a multiplicity held together under the direction
of a divine plan. God creates in order to express His
perfection in a diversity of ways. This means that His
creation must give rise to diverse grades of beings, some
higher and some lower, some more complete, some less
complete than others. What God intends by His creation is
the most perfect <u>order</u> of the things He makes.[15] Hence
the evil which exists in things is something not intended
by God; rather it is a side-effect which must result if
there is to be any creation at all.[16] In other words,
creation is something which can exist only to the extent
that evil accompanies it as a side-effect. That is, either
God creates with some non-intended evil as a side-effect,
or God does not create at all.

The reason for this is simple. For Thomas the only
reason God can have to create is His own goodness. This
desire to express the eminence of His perfection prompts
God to create a diversity of things. He could have created
only one thing, and created it perfectly, but since every
likeness of God falls short of God's goodness, He chose, as
a more perfect form of expression, to create a diversity of
things. This, then, is the plan behind God's creation:
The most perfect order of the things He makes. This is
what He intends or wants. To express His perfection in
diverse ways, however, has, as an invariable consequence,
that God create likenesses of Himself of diverse orders
and grades. This, in turn, means that among the likenesses
He makes some are more complete than others. With respect
to their incompleteness they lack something they ought to
have, and are called "evil." That is, evil, in a general
and vague way of speaking, is an incompleteness in the
existence of something, and, as such, arises from the
<u>limitedness</u> of what is rather than existence being
in something limited.[17] In other words, what God creates
is that which exists. Evil, on the other hand, is precisely what God does not create. It is an incompleteness
in the things God creates which God permits because this
enables Him most completely and suitably to order the
diversity of things He creates. Evil is what God does not
create; it is that which God's creative act does not bring
to its completion, <u>but could have</u>.[18] Hence our awareness
of evil arises from our understanding that something which
exists does not exist in as complete a manner as it could

have. God could have allowed something to exist in a more complete way, but He did not because the intention behind creation is the best order of a diversity of things, not the making of one thing. This, however, demands that some things exist more completely and perfectly than do others.

It does not appear, then, that the presence of evil in things rules out the existence of God. Rather, the exact reverse appears to be the case. The recognition of evil seems to presuppose an awareness of a providential order. For we are aware of evil only to the extent that we are aware that a thing does not possess something it is entitled to possess, or is supposed to possess. Where, however, does one get this notion of entitlement or supposition from? Why is a person supposed to have hands, or supposed to be healthy, or supposed to treat other people justly? And if a person is not supposed to have, be, or behave thus, why do we say people who are without these are in some respect evil or deficient? The answer does not appear to lie in the fact that we get pleasure from talking this way or because we find it useful to do so because the notions of pleasure and utility are unintelligible apart from the notion of entitlement or supposition. For that which is pleasurable or useful must <u>somehow</u> complete or fulfill a being; but a thing can be fulfilled or completed only to the extent that it possesses something it is suited to possess, meant to have, entitled to, supposed to have, and so on. In other words, it does not appear possible to posit the reality of evil and, at the same time, to deny the reality of an order behind things simply by understanding "good" and "evil" in terms of pleasure and utility. The reason for this is, again, that even these notions are unintelligible without some awareness of a providential order in things.

The problem, then, appears to be not how can God exist if there is evil in the world. The problem appears to be how can anyone make an intelligible claim that there is evil in the world unless he recognizes that God exists? For to claim that one encounters evil in the world presupposes that one encounters beings which exist or behave in a manner that goes counter to some order and direction imposed on them by another.

Thomas's response to the second objection raised in

in this article is something which needs little elaboration on our part. To those who would claim that everything which happens in the physical world can be fully explained either by physical causes or man's intellect and will, Thomas has this reply. One cannot explain physical operations on the basis of physical causes alone because there is nothing within the nature of a physical thing, devoid as it is of any decision-making faculty, which can account for the orderly and mostly self-benefitting direction of its operations.

In addition, man-caused events must depend on a higher cause than man's powers of intellect and will for these powers are changeable; they only operate when activated by another. Hence they must ultimately depend for their operation on a first immobile and _per se_ necessary being.[19]

CONCLUSION

At the beginning of this work we described our intention to write a simplified introduction to St. Thomas because we considered such a work to be needed to help solve some of the problems we all face today. Above all else, we have tried to remain faithful, throughout the book, to the teachings of St. Thomas. We commented in the beginning about Thomas's sense of order, his keen metaphysical insight, his clear understanding of the nature and scope of human learning, and, in particular, about his wisdom. We have tried to give instances of these features we find in St. Thomas by examining his views on philosophy, on man, and on God. In each of these areas we see Thomas manifesting all the characteristics we have attributed to him.

No doubt there may be objections which some readers might have to Thomas's positions on the diverse issues we have examined. They may feel that they have good reason to doubt what Thomas has to say on one matter or another. To such readers we would like to say this. In this work we have consciously tried to avoid being polemical. We have tried mainly to give a simplified exposition of points of Thomas's teaching which one needs to know before one can do advanced work in Thomas. At the same time, we have tried to show, in a simplified way, why it is reasonable to look at philosophy, man and God the way St. Thomas does. In a work such as this we do not think it suitable to defend Thomas's position against other thinkers or against a host of arguments. That is not the purpose of the work. At the beginning of this work we said we believed St. Thomas to be wiser than any thinker in the history of philosophy. Certainly we could be wrong about this. We frequently make mistakes. So it would not be the first time we found ourselves confused about something. In addition, even if we are right this does not mean that the way St. Thomas looks at philosophy is the only way to look at philosophy, or that St. Thomas has said all that there is to be said in philosophy. All that we have tried to do in this work has been to make available to a wider audience what we consider to be important

parts of the wisdom of St. Thomas. And we have tried to
show why the positions Thomas takes are reasonable ones to
take. Having done this, this does not mean that we think
there are no other ways of considering the issues we have
considered, or that we have exhausted the corpus
philosophiae. So to those readers who find themselves troub-
led by Thomas's views, we would like to say this. Go to
Thomas. Read him in an objective way, the way you might
read any other thinker. Try to understand what he is
really saying, and try to argue against him. Put him to the
test on your own, and do so as objectively as you can. Only
after doing this will you be able to appreciate the power
of this man and the wisdom of this saint.

PART 1

CHAPTER I

Questions for Study and Discussion:

1. What was the general atmosphere of education surrounding St. Thomas as a teenager?

2. What did St. Thomas study at the University of Naples? Under whom?

3. When was the Order of Preachers established? By Whom?

4. How did Thomas's family react to his decision to become a Dominican? Why?

5. How did Thomas, as far as we know, spend the years 1248-1256?

6. Describe the structure and degree requirements of the University of Paris when Thomas was there. Under whom did Thomas matriculate at the University of Paris?

7. What was the principium?

8. What was a cursor biblicus?

9. What was the Sentences of Peter Lombard? Why was it important?

10. What were the two methods of teaching used at the medieval university? How did they develop?

11. What is Scholasticism?

12. What was the source of the friction between the secular clergy and the mendicants in the 1230's through the 1250's?

13. Who was William of St. Amour? How was he connected with the anti-mendicant movement?

14. Describe the life of Thomas between 1256-1268.

15. Why does Father Weisheipl say that what Thomas accomplished between 1269-1273 "defies imitation"?

16. What peculiar incidents happened after the death of St. Thomas?

CHAPTER II

Questions for Study and Discussion:

1. What was, perhaps, the major issue of medieval Christian philosophy?

2. Explain, in a general way, St. Thomas's view of the acquisition of knowledge.

3. What are the four divisions of speculative philosophy or science for St. Thomas?

4. What is the subject of scientific learning for St. Thomas?

5. What are the liberal arts? Why are they called "liberal arts?"

6. How is one speculative science distinguished by St. Thomas from another?

7. What is abstractio? separatio? How are these applied in the various divisions of speculative philosophy?

8. What does St. Thomas mean by abstractio totius? abstractio formae?

9. Explain the meaning of "sensible matter" and "intelligible matter."

10. Recount Thomas's explanation of "intermediate science."

11. Why, for St. Thomas, is metaphysics the highest degree intellectual?

12. Describe the different methods of reasoning Thomas finds involved in the speculative sciences.

13. What is the subject matter of metaphysics for St. Thomas?

14. What is the difference between religious Faith and theology for St. Thomas?

15. Why would St. Thomas think that Faith perfects rather than distorts philosophy?

CHAPTER III

Questions For Study and Discussion:

1. What is the five-fold division of the physical world for Aristotle?

2. Why does Aristotle consider one level of physical reality to be "higher" or superior to another?

3. What does Aristotle mean by "essence"? "accident"?

4. What are the three conditions of physical change for Aristotle? Why is physical change unintelligible without these conditions?

5. What are the four causes of change? Explain what they mean.

6. How does St. Thomas reconcile Aristotle's view of change with the Christian teaching on creation?

CHAPTER IV

Questions for Study and Discussion:

1. Why would it be misleading to look at St. Thomas as an Aristotelian philosopher?

2. How does St. Thomas's view of "being" differ from Aristotle's?

3. What does Thomas mean by "essence"? "_esse_"?

4. What does Thomas mean by "active" and "passive" power?

5. For St. Thomas how does the way a thing operates indicate the way it possesses the act-of-existing?

6. What are the different ways Thomas thinks we use words when talking about reality? Explain.

7. Why does St. Thomas think the term "being" expresses an analogous concept?

8. What are transcendental characteristics of being? Enumerate and explain each of the transcendentals.

PART 2

CHAPTER I

Questions for Study and Discussion:

1. What was the theological and philosophical context within which St. Thomas worked when developing his view of human nature?

2. Recount St. Thomas's objections to the position of Averroes.

3. Explain how Thomas shows a spiritual substance can be united to a body.

4. Why does St. Thomas contend that the soul's operation of understanding can be performed independently of matter?

5. Why does St. Thomas consider the soul to be immortal? Explain.

CHAPTER II

Questions for Study and Discussion:

1. What are the two different kinds of objects of operations? What kind of power corresponds to each?

2. What does it mean to say that the soul is related to the body according to "a transcendent order of freedom"?

3. Describe the soul's relationship to the body on the level of vegetative life.

4. Describe the soul's relationship to the body on the level of sense life.

5. Describe the soul's relationship to the body on the level of intellectual life.

CHAPTER III

Questions for Study and Discussion:

1. List and explain several of the principles which dominate St. Thomas's understanding of philosophy, metaphysics and man.

2. Why, for Thomas, is the moral life the distinctively free life of the human person?

3. What does St. Thomas mean by "natural law"? "eternal law"? and "divine law"?

4. Relate St. Thomas's teaching on creation and providence to his teaching on natural law.

5. What is the ultimate human happiness for St. Thomas? Why is natural law insufficient to obtain this?

6. According to St. Thomas, how is man made good? How is man's good achieved?

7. Explain why St. Thomas thinks grace and providence perfect rather than destroy human freedom.

PART 3

CHAPTER I

Questions for Study and Discussion:

1. What are some positions rejected by St. Thomas regarding the possibility of proving God's existence?

2. What does St. Thomas understand by the term "self-evident"?

3. What does St. Thomas hold, on the one hand, that we cannot know what God is, but that we can know that God is?

4. How might St. Thomas respond to the teaching of St. Anselm regarding the self-evidence of God's existence?

5. Explain the meaning of the terms "certain," "opinion," "doubt," and "faith."

6. In what way, for St. Thomas, do God's effects "resemble" God?

7. Explain the difference between a demonstration propter quid and a demonstration quia.

CHAPTER II

Questions for Study and Discussion:

1. What is the central link in St. Thomas's demonstration for God's existence?

2. How does one recognize the distinction in sensible things between essence and existence?

3. List the general outline Thomas has in mind as he approaches his demonstration.

4. What is the starting point of Thomas's demonstration quia for God's existence?

5. Explain Thomas's "first way." What does Thomas mean by "motion" here? Why is the length of the world's duration of no importance to St. Thomas here? Why cannot there be an infinite series of movers in essential subordination one to another?

6. Explain the "second way." Why is this "way" more abstract than the "first way"?

7. Explain the "third way." Why, for St. Thomas, is it necessary that one who denies God's existence should hold that at sometime in the past there was nothing in existence?

8. Explain Thomas's "fourth way." How does this way follow a definite order of learning intended to have a reader feel reverance and admiration of God's power?

9. Explain the "fifth way."

10. How would St. Thomas respond to the objection that God cannot exist because the world is a self- explaining fact?

11. How would St. Thomas reply to the objection that God cannot exist because there is evil in the world?

ENDNOTES

INTRODUCTION

1 G. K. Chesterton, The Everlasting Man (New York: Doubleday and Co., Inc., 1955), p. 11.

2 Martin Heidegger, An Introduction to Metaphysics, trans. R. Manheim (New Haven: Yale University Press, 1959), p. 42.

3 On this see Henry B. Veatch's, Two Logics (Evanston: Northwestern University Press, 1969), pp. 3-25.

4 See, for instance, St. Thomas Aquinas, Summa contra gentiles, Book I, Chapter 1, trans. Anton C. Pegis (Notre Dame and London: University of Notre Dame Press, 1975), p. 59. Hereafter referred to as S.c.g., I, i, p. 59.

5 Mortimer J. Adler, Aristotle for Everybody: Difficult Thought Made Easy (New York: Macmillan Publishing Co., Inc., and London: Collier Macmillan Publishers, 1978), ix.

6 See endnote n. 4 above.

7 Henry B. Veatch, Aristotle: A Contemporary Appreciation (Bloomington and London: Indiana University Press, 1974), pp. 4-5. Professor Veatch makes this reference about Aristotle, but we think it is likewise applicable to Aquinas.

PART 1

CHAPTER I

1 James A. Weisheipl, O.P., Friar Thomas D'Aquino: His Life, Thought and Work (New York: Doubleday and Co., Inc., 1974), pp. 4-9.

2 Ibid., pp. 3-6

[3] _Ibid._, pp. 9-14.

[4] _Ibid._, pp. 15-16.

[5] _Ibid._, pp. 14-15 and pp. 20-24.

[6] _Ibid._, pp. 27-26.

[7] _Ibid._, pp. 37-43 and p. 67.

[8] _Ibid._, p. 66. See also Etienne Gilson, _History of Christian Philosophy in the Middle Ages_ (New York: Random House, 1955), pp. 246-248. Weisheipl and Gilson cite different age requirements for a Master. Gilson (_op. cit._, p. 248) says 34. Weisheipl (_op.cit._, p. 101) says 35. We are following Fr. Weisheipl here.

[9] _Friar Thomas D'Aquino: His Life, Thought, and Work_, p. 66.

[10] _History of Christian Philosophy in the Middle Ages_, p. 9.

[11] _Ibid._, p. 128.

[12] _Ibid._, p. 247.

[13] _Ibid._, p. 249.

[14] _Friar Thomas D'Aquino: His Life, Thought and Work_, pp. 80-81.

[15] _Ibid._, p. 83.

[16] _Ibidem_.

[17] _Ibid._, pp. 84-92.

[18] _Ibid._, p. 113.

[19] _Ibid._, p. 110, and pp. 130-139.

[20] _Ibid._, pp. 141-163, and p. 187.

[21] Ibid., pp. 149-153, and Ralph McInerny, St. Thomas Aquinas (Boston G. K. Hall and Co., 1977), p. 22.

[22] Ibid., p. 241.

[23] Ibid., p. 242.

[24] Ibid., p. 241.

[25] Ibid., pp. 295-305.

[26] Ibid., pp. 322.

[27] Ibid., pp. 330-331.

[28] Ibid., p. 331.

CHAPTER II

[1] Ralph McInerny, Thomism in An Age of Renewal (Notre Dame and London: University of Notre Dame Press, 1968), p. 30.

[2] For a lucid explanation of Plato's view of knowledge see A. E. Taylor, The Mind of Plato (Ann Arbor: University of Michigan Press, 1969), pp. 34-72.

[3] St. Thomas Aquinas, Quaestio disputata de veritate, q. 11, a.1. Hereafter referred to as Quaest. disp. de ver., q. 11, a. 1.

[4] History of Christian Philosophy in the Middle Ages, pp. 14-16.

[5] For a history of this problem handled in a masterful way see Etienne Gilson, The Unity of Philosophical Experience (New York: Charles Scribner's Sons, 1965).

[6] St. Thomas Aquinas, The Division and Methods of the Sciences, trans, Armand A. Maurer (Toronto: The Pontifical Institute of Mediaeval Studies, 1963), q. 5, a.1, pp. 6-7, Father Maurer's "Introduction," pp. vi-xl, is enormously helpful for a clear understanding of this work.

[7] Ibid., q. 5, a. 1, Reply to 3, pp. 11-13.

[8] Ibid., q. 5, a. 3, Reply to 5, footnote n. 21, p. 34, St. Thomas did not distinguish between astronomy and astrology. As a medievalist he sees the stars playing a wider role than we see them playing in the influence on everyday life.

[9] See endnote n. 7. above.

[10] The Division and Methods of the Sciences, pp. 28-34.

[11] Ibidem.

[12] Ibidem.

[13] Ibid., q. 5, a. 1, pp. 6-9, and q. 5, a. 3, Reply to 6, pp. 37-38.

[14] Ibid., q. 5, a.1, p. 8.

[15] Ibid., q. 5, a. 1, Reply to 6, p. 16.

[16] Ibidem.

[17] Ibid., q. 5, a. 1, p. 8.

[18] See endnote n. 10 above.

[19] The Division and Methods of the Sciences, "Introduction," pp. X-XIV.

[20] Ibid., q. 5, a. 3, pp. 37-38. For further clarification see Joseph Owens' not so elementary, but nonetheless, scholarly and informative, An Elementary Christian Metaphysics (Milwaukee: The Bance Publishing Co., 1962), pp. 17-56.

[21] St. Thomas Aquinas, In duodecim libros Metaphysicorum Expositio, Prooemium, ed. Cathala Spiazzi, pp. 1-2. Hereafter referred to as In Meta., Prooemium, pp. 1-2.

[22] The Division and Methods of the Sciences, q. 6, a. 1, pp. 55-61.

[23] Ibid., q. 6, a. 1, Reply to 4, p. 65.

[24] St. Thomas Aquinas, On Being and Essence, trans. Armand A. Maurer (Toronto: The Pontifical Institute of Mediaeval Studies, 1968), "Prologue," p. 29.

[25] Friar Thomas D'Aquino: His Life, Thought, and Work, p. 102.

[26] St. Thomas Aquinas, Summa contra gentiles, Book IV, Chapter 1, trans. Charles J. O'Neil (Notre Dame and London; University of Notre Dame Press, 1975), pp. 35-40. Hereafter referred to as S.c.g., IV, 1, pp. 35-40.

[27] S.c.g. I, 5, p. 71.

[28] See endnote n. 26 above.

[29] The Division and Methods of the Sciences, q.5, a.1, Reply to 4, p. 14.

[30] Etienne Gilson, The Christian Philosophy of St. Thomas Aquinas (New York: Random House, 1956), p. 9.

CHAPTER III

[1] Aristotle for Everybody: Difficult Thought Made Easy, p. 6.

[2] Ibid., pp. 8-15.

[3] Ibidem.

[4] Aristotle, Categories, in Richard McKeon ed., The Basic Works of Aristotle (New York: Random House, 1968), 4, 2a, 25-27, p. 3.

[5] Aristotle: A Contemporary Appreciation, pp. 31-39.

[6] Ibid., pp. 41-49.

[7] See On Being and Essence, Ch. 2, n. 4, pp. 34-44, and Aristotle Physics I, 4-9.

[8] W.K.C. Guthrie, The Greek Philosophers: From Thales to Aristotle (New York: Harper and Row, 1960), pp. 16-26.

[9] Ralph McInerny, St. Thomas Aquinas (Boston: G. K. Hall and Co., 1977), pp. 34-38.

CHAPTER IV

[1] On the view that St. Thomas was primarily a theologian see The Christian Philosophy of St. Thomas Aquinas, pp. 3-7.

[2] The Unity of Philosophical Experience, pp. 301-306.

[3] In Meta., Prooemium, ed. Cathala-Sprazzi, pp. 1-2.

[4] Etienne Gilson, The Philosopher and Theology (New York: Random House, 1962), p. 206.

[5] The History of Christian Philosophy in the Middle Ages, pp. 361-383.

[6] For more on this see Etienne Gilson's masterpiece, Being and Some Philosophers, (Toronto: Pontifical Institute of Mediaeval Studies, 1952), pp. 96-107.

[7] For a further consideration of this problem see Mortimer Adler's St. Thomas and the Gentiles (Milwaukee: Marquette University Press, 1948), pp. 7-11.

[8] On Being and Essence, "Prologue," p. 29.

[9] Aristotle, Metaphysics, in the Basic Works of Aristotle, IV, 1, 21-25, p. 731.

[10] The Division and Methods of the Sciences, "Introduction," endnote n. 37, p. xxix.

[11] Ibidem, and On Being and Essence, "Introduction," pp. 13-17.

[12] For a more detailed consideration of this problem see Being and Some Philosophers, pp. 41-51.

[13] Ibid., pp. 72-73.

[14] St. Thomas Aquinas, De potentia Dei, q. 7, a.2, ad 9.

[15] Quaest. disp. de ver., q. 21, a. 4, ad 4.

[16] On Being and Essence, "Introduction," p. 17.

[17] Ibid., ch. 1, n. 2, pp. 29-30.

[18] The Division and Methods of the Sciences, "Introduction," pp. xvii-xxx.

[19] On Being and Essence, ch. 1, n. 4, pp. 31-32.

[20] Ibid., ch. 1, n. 4, p. 31.

[21] Ibid., ch. 1, n. 4, pp. 31-32.

[22] Ibid., ch. 1, n. 4, p. 32.

[23] Ibid., ch. 1, n. 5, pp. 32-33.

[24] The Christian Philosophy of St. Thomas Aquinas, pp. 30-31.

[25] See St. Thomas Aquinas, Scriptum super Libros Senteniarium, I, d. 8, q. 2, a. 2.

[26] S.c.g., I, 22, pp. 118-121.

[27] St. Thomas Aquinas, Summa contra gentiles, Book II, chapter 1, trans. James F. Anderson (Notre Dame and London: University of Notre Dame Press, 1975), p. 29. Hereafter referred to as S. c. g., II, 1, p. 29.

[28] Ibid., II, 2, p. 29.

[29] Ibid., II, 7, p. 38.

[30] Ibidem.

[31] Ibid., I, 16, pp. 100-101.

[32] On Being and Essence, ch. 4, n. 7, pp. 56-57.

[33] Ibid., ch 4, n. 5, p. 55.

[34] S.c.g., I, pp. 143-149. For more on this see James F. Anderson, The Bond of Being (New York: Greenwood Press, 1969).

[35] The Bond of Being, pp. 40-83.

[36] Quaest. disp. de ver. I, 1.

[37] Ibidem.

PART 2

CHAPTER I

[1] Anton C. Pegis, St. Thomas and the Problem of the Soul in the Thirteenth Century (Toronto: Pontifical Institute of Mediaeval Studies, 1976), p. 121.

[2] St. Thomas Aquinas, Quaestion disputata de spiritualibus creaturis, a. 2, Respondeo.

[3] Ibidem.

[4] Ibidem.

[5] Ibidem.

[6] St. Thomas and the Problem of the Soul in the Thirteenth Century, pp. 151 and 201.

[7] Ibid., p. 161.

[8] St. Thomas Aquinas, Quaestio disputata de anima, a. 1, Respondeo. Hereafter referred to as Quaest. disp. de anima, a. 1, Respondeo.

[9] Ibid., a. 11.

[10] Ibidem.

[11] Ibid., a. 14, Respondeo.

162

[12] St. Thomas and the Problem of the Soul in the Thirteenth Century, p. 183.

[13] Ibid., pp. 183-185.

CHAPTER II

[1] S.c.g., I, 1, p. 29.

[2] St. Thomas Aquinas, Summa theologiae, I, q. 77, a. 5. Respondeo. Hereafter referred to as S.t., I, q. 77, a. 5, Respondeo.

[3] Quaest. disp. de anima, a. 11.

[4] S. T., I, q. 77 and q. 78.

[5] Ibidem.

[6] St. Thomas Aquinas, In libros De Anima expositio, II, 14. Hereafter referred to as In II De Anima, 14.

[7] Ibid., 16.

[8] Ibidem.

[9] Ibid., 13.

[10] S. t. I, q. 78.

[11] S. c. g., II, 73, p. 217, and S.t., I, q. 78.

[12] Ibidem.

[13] S.t., I, q. 84, a. 2, Respondeo.

[14] See above pp. 33-36.

[15] S. t., I, q. 84, a. 6, Respondeo.

[16] Ibid., I, q. 84, a. 7. Respondeo.

[17] Ibid., I, q. 85, a. 2, Respondeo.

[18] Ibid., I, q. 16, 2, Respondeo.

CHAPTER III

[1] St. Thomas Aquinas, Summa contra gentiles, Book III trans. Vernon J. Bourke (Notre Dame and London: University of Notre Dame Press, 1975), Part II, chapter 112, p. 115. Hereafter referred to as S. c.g., III, 112, p. 115.

[2] Vernon J. Bourke, "Is Thomas Aquinas A Natural Law Ethicist?," The Monist 58, n. 1 (January 1974), p. 52.

[3] Friar Thomas D'Aquino: His Life, Thought, and Work, p. 249.

[4] "Is Thomas Aquinas A Natural Law Ethicist?," p. 52.

[5] S.c.g., III, 17, p. 73.

[6] Ibid., III, 16, p. 70.

[7] Ibid., III, 97, pp. 66-67.

[8] Ibid., III, 97, pp. 67-68.

[9] Ibid., III, 25, p. 101.

[10] Ibid., III, 48, p. 162.

[11] S.t., I-II, q. 91, a. 2. Respondeo. This and all the English translations from here to the end of the book are from the Blackfriars' edition (New York: McGraw Hill, and London: Eyre and Spottiswood, 1964).

[12] Ibid., I-II, q. 91, a. 4, Respondeo.

[13] Ibid., I-II, q. 91, a. 4 ad 1.

[14] Ibid., S.c.g., III, 113, p. 121.

[15] "Is Thomas Aquinas A Natural Law Ethicist?," p. 61.

[16] S.c.g. III, 116, pp. 125-126.

[17] _Ibid._, III, 118, p. 129.

[18] See above pp. 78-80.

[19] _S. t._, I-II, q. 21, a. 1, Respondeo.

[20] _Ibid._, I-II, q. 94, a. 4, Respondeo.

[21] _S.c.g._ III, 88, pp. 34-35.

[22] St. Thomas Aquinas, _Truth_ (_Quaestiones disputatae de veritate_) vol. III, trans. R. W. Mulligan, J. V. McGlynn, and R. W. Schmidt (Chicago: Henry Regnery Co., 1954), q. 24, a. 1, pp. 137-138.

[23] _S.c.g._, III, 73, p. 244.

[24] _Ibid._, III, 73, p. 245.

[25] _Ibidem._

[26] _Ibid._, III, 150, p. 231.

PART 3

CHAPTER I

[1] On this see Etienne Gilson, _Reason and Revelation in the Middle Ages_ (New York: Charles Scribners Sons, 1938).

[2] St. Anselm, _Proslogium, Monologium_, trans. S. N. Deane (Chicago: Open Court Publishing Co., 1939).

[3] _The Division and Methods of the Sciences_, q. 5, a. 3, Reply, pp. 28-34.

[4] _S. t._, I, q. 2, a., Respondeo.

[5] _Ibid._, I, q. 2, a. 1, ad 1.

[6] _Ibid._, I, q. 2, a. 2. Respondeo.

[7] _Ibid._, I, q. 2, a. 2, ad 3.

[8] Ibid., I, q. 2, a. 2, ob. 1.

[9] Ibid., I, q. 2, a. 2, ad.

[10] Ibid., I, q. 2, a. 2 ob. 3.

[11] Ibid., I, q. 4, a. 3, Respondeo.

[12] Ibid., I, q. 2, a. 2, ob. 2.

[13] For an excellent examination of the difference between the method and goal of the philosopher in contrast to the method and goal of the experimental scientist see Veatch's Two Logics, pp. 3-25.

[14] S. t., I, q. 2, a. 2, Respondeo.

[15] See St. Thomas Aquinas, Sentententia libri Posteriorum Analyticorum, Book I, lect 25. Chapter II

CHAPTER II

[1] S. t., I, q. 2, a. 2, ad 2.

[2] Ibid., I, q. 4, a. 3, Respondeo.

[3] On Being and Essence, ch. 4, n. 7, p. 56.

[4] S. t. I, q. 2, a. 3, Respondeo.

[5] Ibidem.

[6] Ibidem.

[7] St. Thomas Aquinas, In libros De Caelo et Mundo Expositio, I, lect. 29.

[8] S. t. I, q. 2, a. 3, Respondeo.

[9] S. c. g., II, 2, p. 30.

[10] S. t., I, q. 3, a. 5, c.

[11] For more on this see Being and Some Philosophers, pp. 41-51.

[12] _S.t._ I, q. 2, a. 3, Respondeo.

[13] _Ibid._, I. Q. 2, a. 3. ob. 1.

[14] _Ibid._, I, q. 2, a. 3, ob. 2.

[15] _S. c. g._, III, 97, pp. 67-68.

[16] _Ibid._, I, 95, p. 291; II, 41, pp. 122-123; III, pp. 41-69.

[17] _Ibid._, II, 41, pp. 122-123.

[18] _Ibid._, III, 7, p. 48.

[19] _S.t._, I, q. 2, a. 3, ad 2.

SELECT BIBLIOGRAPHY

For anyone wishing to do further study in the work of St. Thomas, we think the following works will be helpful:

Adler, Mortimer J. _St. Thomas and the Gentiles._ Milwaukee: Marquette University Press, 1948.

Anderson, James F. _The Bond of Being._ New York: Greenwood Press, 1969.

Aquinas, St. Thomas. _The Division and Method of the Sciences._ Trans. Armand A. Maurer. Toronto: Pontifical Institute of Mediaeval Studies, 1963. While one might find the text of Aquinas difficult to understand Father Maurer's "Introduction" is very lucid. The work is extremely important for understanding St. Thomas.

----------. _On Being and Essence._ Trans. Armand A. Maurer. Toronto: Pontifical Institute of Mediaeval Studies, 1968. Once again, the text of Aquinas is difficult, if not impossible, for a beginner to understand. Father Maurer's "Introduction," however, is, as usual, enormously helpful for understanding this masterful work.

Clark, Mary T. _An Aquinas Reader._ New York: Doubleday and Co., Inc. Sister Clark's work provides a number of important selections from St. Thomas in clear translation.

Chesterton, Gilbert K. _St. Thomas Aquinas--The Dumb-Ox._ New York: Doubleday and Co., Inc., 1956. Chesterton's account of the life, thought and character of St. Thomas is Chesterton at his best. The work has some historical inaccuracies, however.

Gilson, Etienne H. _Being and Some Philosophers._ Toronto: Pontifical Institute of Mediaeval Studies, 1952. This work is a masterpiece of metaphysical insight.

----------. The Christian Philosophy of St. Thomas Aquinas.
Trans. L. K. Shook, New York: Ramdom House,
1956. This book is a must for the serious student of
St. Thomas, as is practically everything Gilson has
written.

McInerny, Ralph M. St. Thomas Aquinas. Boston: G. K. Hall
and Co., 1977.

----------. Thomism in an Age of Renewal. Notre Dame and
London: University of Notre Dame Press, 1968. This
work is very clearly written and can be very helpful
for a beginner.

Owens, Joseph. An Elementary Christian Metaphysics.
Milwaukee: The Bruce Publishing Co., 1963. An
incomparably rich work, but it is not so elementary.

Phelan, Gerald B. "The Being of Creatures." G. B. Phelan:
Selected Papers. Ed. Arthur G. Kirn. Toronto:
Pontifical Institute of Mediaeval Studies, 1967, 83-94.

----------. "The Existentialism of St. Thomas," Proceedings
of the American Catholic Philosophical Association, 21
(1946), 25-40.

Renard, Henri. "Essence and Existence." Proceedings of the
American Catholic Philosophical Association, 21 (1946),
53-66.

----------. "What is St. Thomas' Approach to Metaphysics?"
New Scholasticism, 30 (1956), 64-83.

Sweeney, Leo. "Essence/Existence in Thomas Aquinas' Early
Writings," Proceedings of the American Catholic
Philosophical Association, 21 (1946), 53-66.

Weisheipl, James A. Friar Thomas D'Aquino: His Life,
Thought, and Work. New York: Doubleday and Co., Inc.,
1974. Contains a wealth of information unavailable in
other works. A must reading for anyone in doing
Thomistic research.

ABOUT THE AUTHOR

Dr. Peter A. Redpath is a graduate of Iona College, New Rochelle, New York. He was a graduate fellow at S.U.N.Y. at Buffalo, from which he received his Ph.D. in 1974. He is currently an Assistant Professor of Philosophy at St. John's University, Staten Island, New York.